Lessons By Heart

Learned at the Feet of Jesus

By Tamara J Benson

LESSONS BY HEART

Learned at the Feet of Jesus

Copyright ©2009 by Tamara J. Benson
All rights reserved

This book is protected by the copyright law of the United States of America. This book may not be copied or reprinted for commercial gain or profit. The use of short quotations or occasional page copying for personal or group study is permitted and encouraged. Permission will be granted upon request.

Unless otherwise noted, all Scripture quotations are from the Holy Bible, New King James Version. Copyright © 1982 by Thomas Nelson, Inc. Used by permission. All rights reserved.

Published by Tamara Benson
Redding, CA 96002

International Standard Book Number: 978-0-578-02735-7

To order more books or to learn more about the author, please visit the author's website:
www.LessonsByHeart.wordpress.com
Or e-mail the author at
batransformed1@yahoo.com

Cover photograph by Stacy Braswell. Used by permission.
Cover design by Juliet King
www.ettaseyes.com

Printed in the United States of America

Dedication

This book is dedicated to my Lord and Savior, Jesus Christ. Without Him this book would not be possible.

...to my husband, Wendel, who encourages me always to take risks and to share with others what I've learned.

...and to my children and grandchildren. God has indeed blessed me with a full quiver. They are: Christian, Beth, Charity, Tyree, Drew, Ted, and Rob; my son-in-law, Brandon; my daughters-in-law, Audrey and Sabrina; and my grandchildren: Toby, Emily, Abby, Eddy, Joshua, Destiny, Rosie & Charlie (the twins!), and Landon. You truly have been gifts to me. Many of life's lessons could not have been learned without you.

Acknowledgements

Without the Lord this book would never have been written. The pages following are lessons given by Him as He has patiently been molding and fashioning me into His likeness. He has a long way to go, but I'm so thankful that He never begins anything He doesn't intend to finish! At just the right time He brought everything together to make this dream become a reality.

Matthew 10:8 reads: "Freely you have received, freely give." In February of 2009 a young man demonstrated his understanding of this scripture when he offered a free class to aspiring authors. He graciously shared his knowledge and wisdom of authorship from raw concepts through to a published book. Aaron McMahon, I will always be grateful for your willingness to share with an open hand what God has given you!

To Beth Moore I am deeply indebted. Through her many Bible studies and books I have learned that life is a series of object lessons which God uses to teach us His will and His ways. Every story of our lives teaches us Truth, if we have the ears to hear! If you've never studied the Word with her, I highly recommend *any* of her studies.

Barbara Clary, you have been a gift to me. The Lord has used you to teach me that it's all about Him, and not about me. Like our Savior, you have reached out and touched this untouchable, bringing life to my dead heart. Thank you for your many hours of counsel, and for teaching me how to hear His voice in the midst of my pain.

I also owe a debt of gratitude to everyone who ever encouraged me to write – high school teachers, college professors, clergy, family, mentors, and friends, too numerous to list here! It took a long time for me to accept your words and to act on them! Thank you for seeing in me what I could not.

Janet Newton, I love your tender heart. You watch over your friends, always on the alert for possibilities for us. At the point where I believed that I'd misunderstood God and would never be writing again, you came along with the magazine, "Enjoy." Your offering led me to Sandi – and the beginning of this great adventure.

To Sandi Tillery I am grateful. You invited me to Aaron's class, an unselfish act by an excellent author. I'm thankful that you didn't keep the book writing class to yourself.

Thanks to Carol Mann for taking the time to edit the manuscript. You were a blessing and an inspiration.

Juliet King, you created the most beautiful book cover ever. Thank you so much for all the time you put into it. You have an eye for the beautiful things in life. I love that about you.

Finally, I'd like to thank my husband, Wendel, for his support and encouragement in this endeavor. He's been patient while I've spent hours "clickety-clacking" away on my laptop and listening to my ramblings. I love you more than you'll ever know!

Foreword

Tami Benson has always had a hunger for God and His Word since I have known her. I've also watched in her life as she experienced many of the stories written here and can testify to her sincere desire to hear and obey the Lord's voice.

The vignettes do not leave room for your denial. When you read and relate to the stories, you can picture yourself doing exactly the same thing. Life is not always gentle, and with the trials it is so comforting to know that wisdom and meaning can come from our most difficult times. When I read "Pearls" it brought new meaning to our irritations, and how it gives great value to them as well!

You can read these stories with confidence that Tami has written them from her heart and she is always open to your comments. That is what is seen here, that she is teachable and listening to what the Lord wants to say to her, as well as what she can pass on to others. Read these with your heart and see if the Lord does not speak to you also.

Enjoy!

Barbara Clary

TABLE OF CONTENTS

Introduction	2
Lessons From Heaven	3
Lessons From Sunday School	18
Lessons In Time	34
Lessons Of Life	50
Lessons In Marriage	65
Lessons From Family	79
Lessons In Identity	90
Lessons From Deep In My Heart	101
Lessons To Remember	110
Lessons Of Beauty	121

Introduction

Welcome to my heart. It's a little messy in here, but please make yourself at home. Perhaps you will find furniture in each room that feels familiar.

My prayer is that these short lessons stir something inside your own heart, or bring to mind a lesson Papa had for you that was overlooked. The world in which we live runs at such a frantic pace that the quiet voice of God is easily drowned out.

Everything in life is meant to be a lesson for us. I firmly believe this. It has been a delight to discover just how relevant the Scriptures are to our lives today as I've seen how they apply to everyday events.

Sit back, kick off your shoes, and relax for a bit. Listen with your heart. My prayer is that you will hear echoes of your own lessons as you read through these pages.

Above all, may you be drawn to our Father's heart. He loves you so much that He can't take His eyes off you! He created you for His good pleasure, and longs to join you in fellowship…not just on Sunday morning, but every moment of every day.

You'll soon see what I mean.

"God rewrote the text of my life when I opened the book of my heart to His eyes." (Psalm 18:24, The Message)

- 1 -

Lessons From Heaven

Do You Know My Jesus?

AT FIRST HE SEEMED aloof and untouchable. He had "presence," a demeanor that spoke of great confidence. I watched as he interacted with those around me. There was a kind word here, a thoughtful gesture there. That smile…! I found myself drawn to him. What would it take to get him to notice me? I waited, watched, and hoped. Nothing.

Finally, in a moment of desperation, I boldly spoke to him. He barely seemed to notice, as he turned and left. However, bit-by-bit he began to turn his attention to me. I became the object of his kindness. The more I knew him, the more I wanted to know him. We were married 18 months later!

Imagine how differently things would have turned out had I only sought to know more *about* him. I could have gone to his friends and gathered all kinds of information: What was he like? Where did he live? What did he like and dislike?

What was his history? I could have learned enough to write a book about him without ever knowing him personally.

God says, " you will seek Me and find Me when you search for Me with all your heart. And I will be found by you..." (Jeremiah 29:13, 14a). Jesus says, "If you have seen Me you have seen the Father." (John 14:9).

Too often I have approached the Word from a scientific viewpoint. I wanted to get the facts right...analyze it...verify it. I wanted to know all about the Author: His likes and dislikes, where He lived, what He was like.

However, suppose I wrote a love letter to my husband. When he received it, instead of cherishing it as a token of my love, he memorized it so he could quote it accurately. Then he analyzed it so he could be sure that it was from me. Having proven its authenticity, he then applied it to his friends lives. The one thing he didn't do was to stop and take my words to heart as something I meant specifically *for him*.

If this is what he did with a love letter from me, I would be horrified and deeply wounded. So why do I handle God's letter to me (the Bible) like this? Yes, these other things have value in their place, but His greatest desire is that I should *know* Him, and He *can* be known!

That deep longing in our hearts to love and be loved, know and to be known, is an echo of the Father's heart for us. In His words from Jeremiah, "You will seek Me and find Me when you search for Me with all your heart," can you hear the longing in the words? He *wants* to be sought out. He *wants* to be found. He *wants* to be known – by *us!!*

The good news is that He is waiting for us to invite Him. "Behold, I stand at the door and knock. If *any* (woman) hear my voice and will open the door I will come into (her) and dine with (her) and (she) with Me." Revelation 3:20. He is waiting with great longing just on the other side of the door.

This is not merely a call to salvation, but to intimacy with our Lord. It is the most satisfying relationship we will ever enter into.

The dinner reservations have been made. Will you join Him?

"TOTALLY FREE" INTERNET

THAT'S WHAT IT STATED on the sign just above the CDs at the department store. That's what it said on the CD's package. Believing the old adages, "*you don't get something for nothing*" and "*if it seems too good to be true, it is,*" I looked the package over one more time. There *had* to be a string attached somewhere.

We've all received disks in the mail that offer "up to 700 hours free access." You know the ones. You have to install it, connect to their website and register. Then you must give a credit card or bank account they can access for payment "just in case" you want their service after your free trial. Then, and only then, can you actually begin using this "free" gift. Should you fail to cancel service before the end of your trial you are billed for the next month in advance. The first month is free, but after that it costs you!

I checked the package (again) and found nothing that indicated a required payment, so I took it and headed for my car. I kept looking over my shoulder, expecting security guards at any second. I was so certain that there *had* to be a catch! It was too good to be true.

At home it was time to install the software. While waiting for the computer to boot, I carefully looked over the package again, as well as the CD. There was nothing in fine print so I inserted the CD.

During installation one of the dialog boxes required the selection of a telephone number to use for future connections. Aha! <u>This</u> was where they got you! I wrote down the available telephone numbers, aborted the installation process, and called the operator. I gave her the phone numbers and she stated that these were local calls if the calls were placed from the telephone I was using to talk to her. No charge? No charge.

Still unconvinced by the "totally free" claim, I went back to the computer and installed the software. I kept waiting for the catch. At last, I sat looking at a web browser – and hadn't had to give any surety for payment. It *was* totally free!!

We've been victims of so many cons and scams (or know someone who has) that we find the word "free" hard to believe.

Take eternity, for instance. The Bible says, "the wages of sin is death; but the *gift* of God is eternal life through Jesus Christ our Lord (Romans 6:23).

We look at the offer and search for the fine print. It says "free," but there *has* to be a catch. We don't believe it.

If I had tried to give a credit card number for payment during the software installation, I'd have had a problem. There was no provision for me to enter one. They didn't want payment. It *was* a gift.

The same holds true with God. We sit here with our plan of how we're going to "purchase" His gift, but He has made no provision for us to offer our payment. He didn't need to. It is – as stated – totally free!

Did the department store want something in exchange for the free Internet access? Yes. It was a marketing strategy to increase their sales. Does God want something in exchange for His free gift? Yes. He wants to increase His kingdom. In 2 Peter 3:9 we read, "The Lord is not slack concerning His promise, as some count slackness, but is long-suffering toward us, not willing that any should perish but that *all* should come to repentance."

If you've already received your "totally free" Heaven access, then make copies of the software and distribute them to everyone you encounter. "Freely you have received, freely give" (Matthew 10:8). There are no copyrights on His software. Tell everyone about your Great Provider – be His best advertisement! "And the things that you have heard from me among many witnesses, commit these to faithful men who will be able to teach others also" (2 Timothy 2:2).

Accept no imitations! There is only *one* Provider that will give you access to Heaven. That is Jesus Christ. "I am the way, the truth, and the life. No one comes to the Father *except through me*" (John 14:6). (*Italics mine*)

PS

Although I've used the free Internet access for a while, I still look for the catch. Having had free God-access for much longer, I've finally found the fine print. It states that there is absolutely no charge for the "service" – and Jesus signed it with His own blood. "Knowing that you were not redeemed with corruptible things, like silver or gold, from your aimless conduct received by tradition from your fathers, but with the precious blood of Christ..." (1 Peter 1:18,19).

Pass it on.

EARNED LOVE

OFTEN TIMES, PEOPLE WILL do things for you and then announce that you "owe" them (love, attention, affection, time, etc.). These things weren't done from a pure heart, but with a hidden agenda. It's the old, "I gave to you, now you owe me" thing. This can turn a relationship into a form of prostitution – services bought and paid for.

We do this with God. We teach, feed the poor, volunteer time or goods, etc. in an effort to gain favor with God. After we've given, we go to God with our hand out and say, "OK, now You have to pay me in love." He sadly shakes His head and says, "It was a gift." He doesn't withhold, but the pay-off isn't what we wanted, so we try something else and then go back to God. With tender compassion He states, "It was free."

On and on it goes. We strive in every way imaginable – to no avail.

At long last we give up. We've come to the end of ourselves and realize we have nothing to offer. That's when He scoops us into His everlasting arms. He smoothes our hair, hugs us close, and sighs, "Finally! I've loved you all along. You were so busy trying to earn my love that you've never taken the time to get to know me. If you had, you would have realized long ago how very much I love you!"

Deuteronomy 33:27 "The Eternal God is a dwelling place, and underneath are the everlasting arms..."

DO YOU TRUST ME?

"I HAVE AN OPPORTUNITY to showcase my skills at an upcoming Expo. Thousands of people will witness this. It's the chance of a lifetime. Will you be my model?" your best friend asks.

"Well...what do I have to do?" (Uncertain whether to agree or not.)

"I'd like for you to allow me to create a new hairstyle. It will be unique. You'll love the end result," is the reply.

"What are you gonna do to me?" you ask, winding a piece of your waist-length hair around your finger.

"Oh...cut, perm, tint. It'll be fabulous. You'll see. You're perfect for what I have in mind. No one else will do. Will you trust me?" A loaded question!

What would you do? This is your best friend. A lot is at stake – your friendship & your looks!

Believe it or not, this is similar to God and Abraham. (It's rather a simplistic example, I know!)

In Genesis 22, God wanted to give Abraham a makeover. Instead of his looks, God was (as He always is) after Abraham's heart...

...and a lot was at stake!

Could Abraham trust God? It was a lot to ask of a "friend"...to sacrifice that which he loved above all else – Isaac...

To turn his Friend away would be to put a rift between them. But to agree – that could cost him his son. What if things didn't work out? The faith he had in God would vanish. Should he do it? Could he do it? Abraham's mind must have been a veritable whirlwind.

Finally, drawing upon memories of the miracles he'd been a witness of – and a party to – he resolved to take his prized possession and be the model his Lord was asking them to be.

The Bible says, "and the Scripture was fulfilled which says, 'And Abraham believed God, and it was reckoned to him as righteousness,' and he was called the friend of God." (James 2:23)

The friend of God; truly Abraham was, for he agreed to have God use him to showcase His grace by sparing Abraham's son. At the same time, they modeled the sacrifice of God's own Son on that very hill – a sacrifice that would provide His grace for all who would receive it.

"For by grace you have been saved through faith, and that not of yourselves, it is the gift of God; not of works, so that no one may boast." (Eph. 2: 8,9)

What is there, in your own life, that God is asking you to bring to the altar? What do you love above God? Pride? Self-righteousness? Is it things? House? Car? Money? Are you hanging on to it for dear life? Is it causing a rift between you and the Lord?

This is our call to step out...put our actions where we claim to have faith. Our hearts are purified when our actions finally match our words.

To talk the talk is a cinch – go to any church and we see how easily people can do this. Ah, but to REALLY act on what we say we believe – that's when it gets tough!

The Lord asks, "Do you trust Me?

THE GLORY OF GOD

THE WHOLE EARTH IS full of His glory (Isaiah 6:3). I discovered this in my own yard last spring.

It all began with my "Jonah" corner. I got the landscape idea from a Florida resort where their decorative ground cover was seashells – tons of them. I loved the effect and decided to use it at home. After it was done, I realized that the next time I decided to run in the opposite direction from where God was leading I should visit my little corner and remind myself that it really *stinks* inside the big fish (Book of Jonah)!

The sand dollars in my "Jonah" corner are representatives of the wounds of Jesus and the peace of God (they have doves inside them).

The Jasmine's fragrance tells of the aroma of the prayers of the saints (Revelation 5:8). The Purple-Robed Locust tree, towering over the house, is a reminder of the majesty of God (Job 37:22). The Trumpet vine causes me to long for the sounding of the last trump...the one calling us home (1 Thessalonians 4:16).

In the back yard, I planted a Japanese Lantern tree. During its first winter, the top broke off in the wind. Not wanting to hassle with digging it up and replacing it, I waited for it to get several shoots. I chose the three strongest ones and braided them together. Later, I realized that "the braiding effect" was symbolic of Ecclesiastes 4:12, which reads, "a cord of three strands is not quickly broken." We now refer to it as the "marriage" tree – husband, wife, and God. In late summer it gets pagoda-shaped clusters of pale yellow flowers at the top. Just as Jesus is the light of the world, so a Godly marriage shines out to a lost and dying world (Matthew 5:16).

Rocks are plentiful and remind me that Jesus is my Rock (1 Corinthians 10:4). The bees serve to draw my thoughts to God's Word...sweet as honey on my lips (Psalm 19:10). Hummingbirds stir a longing for the millennium when I will be able to hold them!

The small gate is a reminder that the way to heaven is narrow (Matthew 7:14). Whom do I know that is not a believer, and that I can pray for?

The many bulb flowers tell of the life, death, and resurrection of my Lord (1 Corinthians 15:3,4). Their return every year speaks of His faithfulness (Lamentations 3:23). The bougainvillea (which isn't supposed to grow in our area) demonstrates God's ability to do the impossible (Mark 10:27).

A beautiful Lotus adds vibrant color. It has three flame shaped flowers per cluster that are yellow at the base and gradually change to deep orange at the tips. These recall the Tri-unity and justice of God (Psalm 89:14).

Moss roses are great! They get new blossoms every day. They are a reminder that God's mercies are also new every day (Lamentations 3:22, 23). There are yellow Gazanias: symbolic of the Son who was sacrificed so that I might live with Him forever (Hebrews 9:28).

Due to a wayward child, I planted rose bushes under the bedroom windows. I chose red because they were pretty. Now I see that these also represent the cross where Jesus shed his blood for my sins; the thorns are a reminder of the crown He wore while hanging there, where I should have been.

One plant I selected was the Passion Vine. It has such unusual flowers. Later I found that they were so named because each component speaks of Christ – 10 petals for 10 of the faithful disciples, the five stamens represent the five wounds, and the lacy crown is a reminder of His deity.

The sheltering trees remind me that we are in the shadow of His wing (Psalm 17:8).

Ah, but then I did a foolish thing. I planted mint. It was nice to the touch, delightful to smell, lovely to taste, refreshing even. I carelessly planted a few pieces. Two years later, I had to labor many days to remove it from the place where I had planted it...as well as the walkway, back yard, front yard, and my neighbor's yard!!! It makes me think of what the Bible calls a "besetting sin." (Hebrews 12:1) It seems innocent enough at the time. It piques all the senses, but once it takes hold, it requires diligence to dig it out. The roots run rampant and its troublesome shoots spring up in many unexpected places.

I wasn't satisfied with just one "sin." I also planted three clumps of bamboo. I'm still dealing with the consequences!

One tree out front is the strangest looking thing. We call him "Hairy." He is staked up, but hangs to the ground. This poor thing was meant to be ground cover, but I wanted a tree there. After several years, his looks haven't improved any. He looks awkward and out of place. He stands as a reminder of what happens when I try to do things that only God is qualified to do. He is an unshapely, awkward mess that is not serving his purpose (nor speaking well of the one who "fashioned" him). Some things are best left up to God (Philippians 3:21).

I could go on and on, but you get the idea.

The thing that amazes me is that none of this was done on purpose. The significance occurred to me only after it was completed. Even that is like the cross. No one understood the significance of His activities until after Jesus claimed, "It is finished." (John 19:30)

MERRY CHRISTMAS

THE AD READ, "NATIVITY SET complete with crèche, Mary, Joseph and the baby." The *baby?* Doesn't He have a name?

That's funny because without "the baby," Mary and Joseph have no significance. They are just another couple having a baby – no different than you or I. They become just another poor family, giving birth amongst the animals because they have nowhere to go. They come, they go, they slip off the pages of history...just like everyone else.

What do we really know about Mary or Joseph? We know next to nothing of their upbringing, their families (did they have siblings?), their education, or their accomplishments. Without "the baby," there is nothing to recommend them, to make them stand out from anyone else.

Without "the baby," there is no real reason to have a "happy holiday." After all the word "holiday" is actually the two words, "holy day," combined. For whom else would we have a holy day to commemorate? Santa? Probably not.

More to the point, we need to realize that without "the baby" *none* of us has significance. What would make us a distinct person; different than any other, if we just lived our short lives, died, and ceased to exist? What would be the purpose behind giving, loving, caring, or otherwise take care of anyone else's needs? If this life is all we have, then why not get all we can while we can? Most of the world believes this...and look at how they live. "Give me more, bigger, brighter, better," is their cry. They spend thousands annually on unnecessary gadgets and gizmos – and scoff at the homeless, the downtrodden, and the helpless.

The most important name of all is *Jesus.* He makes *all* the difference. He is the reason that our world has not imploded. There are enough people still bearing His name and being obedient to His will to keep us from total ruin. With the hope of an eternity with Jesus, they pray for those around them, taking His *name* to them, offering them the same hope that they themselves have.

The most important name of all is *Jesus. He* commands us to love our neighbor as ourselves. He calls us to live beyond ourselves, to sacrifice for others, as we get involved in their lives. When asked why we do what we do the door is opened for us to share the Good News and the *Name* of the One who died for them.

The most important name of all is *Jesus.* Without Him we have no future. We have no hope. We live; we die, and then slip off the pages of history, most without leaving so much as a ripple in the pond of life.

Let the rest of the world have a "happy holiday." As for me and my house, we will have a MERRY *CHRIST*MAS! Moreover, wish one to everyone else, "politically correct" or not! We have a lot to celebrate!!!

"...you shall call His name **JESUS**, *for He will save His people from their sins.*" Matthew 1:2

- 2 -

Lessons From Sunday School

PEARLS

IMAGINE WHAT A SURPRISE the first pearl discovery must have been. It was most remarkable, to be sure; such a beautiful find in a most unlikely place. As they held it up to the light, no doubt they were awestruck at the hues of purple, gold, and blue that shimmered from its surface.

Isn't that what life is like? In the midst of some of the ugliest circumstances, we discover little nuggets of beauty.

Like the pearls of a beautiful necklace, so are the days of our lives. During our stay on earth, we are given a series of object lessons. As they are strung together, they become our adornment – not unlike a strand of pearls.

When we hold them up to the Light, we find the fingerprints of Jesus – purple, and gold, and blue – all over them!

The favorite color of pearl is white. This is true whether it is a literal pearl, or a spiritual one. These represent the "white" days of our lives. Everything was good, we were well behaved, and we learned from these times.

The next favored ones are cream-colored and yellow. These are the "little bit naughty" days. If they're the best we have, we will "wear" these and show them off.

Another variety of pearls are pink. These are the days when we didn't wear red – but probably could have! Not everyone wants others to know that they own "pink" pearls.

Gray pearls might represent illness or depression. Although still beautiful, they lack the sparkle of the others.

Black pearls are usually not the first choice. I'm not sure why. I have a strand of these and I love them. They represent the dark days of our lives: death, destruction, or maybe depths of despair.

The thing I admire about black pearls, however, is that they best reflect the hues of God – purple, and gold, and blue! With or without light, the colors are easily seen.

So it is with the dark days of our lives. As we look back over them it is often most easy to see God's hand at work.

There are also two types of pearl: those from the ocean and those from fresh water. The ocean pearls are nearly perfect orbs, while those from fresh water are knobby and asymmetrical. The difference could be the difference in the amount of salt content in the water.

These two types could be considered situations handled in submission to God (saltwater), or in our own strength (fresh water). When we go through a trial or event and are fully dependent on God, the outcome is nearly perfect. On the other hand, when we try to handle these on our own the end result is usually awkward and misshapen. Of course, when we finally cry out to God, He comes along and helps us through, still leaving His fingerprints on the finished product!

Our Master Craftsman has provided us with a variety of pearls with which to adorn ourselves. Most of us are now in possession of "pearls" in every color of the rainbow. They are for our learning, and to share the wisdom we've received with younger women (Titus 2:4).

Let's invite the Lord to teach us the wisdom He provided in each pearl of our lives. While no two pearls are identical, *we* don't want a whole strand of similar-looking ones. Jewelers will look for nearly identical ones for necklaces, but we are not jewelers! Matching pearls mean we're repeating the same trial – and haven't learned the lesson yet!

Pearls, in Scripture, refer to wisdom (Matthew 7:6). That's what we should acquire from every event of our lives. Our own history, like that of people of the Old Testament, is there for our learning (Romans 15:4) if we will but have ears to hear. Let's not allow a single trial or test to be wasted, but determine to learn the lessons God has for us in them.

Having learned from our pearls, let us adorn ourselves with the wisdom we've been given, and then teach others how to find God's fingerprints for themselves.

You can't miss them...they're purple, and gold, and blue!

WRITTEN BY GOD'S FINGER

THE LAST PART OF Exodus 31:18 ends with this phrase, "written with the finger of God." This brings to mind a verse in the New Testament that says, "All scripture is *God breathed*. It suddenly occurred to me that if I fully grasped this truth, I would treat the Bible very differently.

The difference between the God of Israel and the gods of every other religion in the world is that He is the One True God. He is real...they are fiction. He is the only God who seeks to lead and guide His people, leaving them in a much better state at the end than they were at the beginning.

"...What other god is there that speaks continually of its love for all of humanity? What other god is there that seeks sacrifice and service for the benefit of the people, and not for its own selfish pleasure? What other god seeks out the individual for the sake of restoration and forgiveness? Show me *one* that is merciful and gracious, longsuffering, and abounding in goodness and truth, keeping mercy for thousands, forgiving iniquity and transgression, and sin, by no means clearing the guilty." (Exodus 34:6,7)

This morning as I read that little phrase, "written with the finger of God," I realized that I have yet to comprehended the immense gift I have received.

How often *this* God has stooped to intervene in my own life! How often I have seen His hand in my circumstances. He has led me, guided me into truths that have been life altering, fed and clothed me, healed me from fatal illness, and so much more. He has been evident in every aspect of my life, and brought a lot of good from so many ugly things in and around me.

I have seen Him work all things together for my good!

Many times I've heard people state that Bible is full of contradictions and has been rewritten so many times that it no longer resembles the original copies. It takes all the self-control I can get my hands on to keep from laughing out loud. The more I study it, the more fascinated I am by how tightly it all fits together. I am an avid reader; and I've never found another book that even comes close to the dynamics of the Bible.

God gives details and when He does, they tie into the rest of the Scripture perfectly.

An excellent example of this is the two fellows in prison with Joseph. They were a cupbearer and a baker. Now why weren't they a tailor and a farmer or some other occupation? If we take a moment to consider these occupations, we soon realize that a baker bakes bread, right? A cupbearer would then do what? What's in the cup this fellow bears for the king, if not wine? Bread and wine; hmmm, that reminds me of something I heard in the New Testament...like at Passover when Jesus was speaking to His disciples about His upcoming death!

"Well, OK. These fellows seem to resemble communion, but isn't this a little contrived?" you might ask. Let's see. When the cupbearer told his dream and Joseph interpreted it, the fellow had reason to rejoice. He would be returning to work in three days. The baker, encouraged by this interpretation, told his dream. Too bad for him; he would be put to death in three days.

The cupbearer lives, the baker would be put to death. Through the blood of Jesus we have eternal life; but *his body was broken for us!*

Not only did the baker die, but *he was broken* through execution. Wow! What a "coincidence!" I love what Chuck Missler says, "coincidence is not a kosher word!"

This is only one story. Jesus told us that the entire Bible was written of Him (Hebrews 10:7, cf. Psalm 40:7). That means that He is in every story.

As I read the Old Testament, I look for Him, like a miner seeks for gold.

He can be found in the scarlet cord that hung from Rahab's window that brought her salvation, just as Christ hanging from the cross brought us ours.

He is in Isaac's story – the son who willingly permitted himself to be sacrificed by His father. Fortunately for Abraham, there was a substitute provided. God was not to be spared this great pain.

Do you know that in Psalms when we read, "salvation," many of the times the word in the original language is, "jeshua"? Jesus? Really? Yep! He's everywhere!!!

Lord, help me to truly grasp the Bible, its great worth, its importance in my life and the life of others. I only caught a glimpse this morning – and only for an instant. May that instant become sustained longer and longer each time I meditate on the treasure that I possess in Your Word.

In Jesus' Name

AMEN!!

\o/

PSALM 139

THE 139TH PSALM is one of my favorites – probably because it's all about me. Don't laugh! You probably love it because it's all about you, too!!

It starts like this:

Lord, You have searched me and known me. You know when I sit and when I rise. You understand my thoughts from afar off. You comprehend my path and my lying down and are acquainted with all my ways. For there is not a word on my tongue but behold, O Lord, You know it all together.

Basically, this says we don't move a muscle (including our tongues) that God is not aware of. We are told in the Bible that He keeps our tears in bottles and knows exactly how many hairs are on our heads! Even more, He is aware of our desires, motives, and our thoughts.

It goes on to say:

"You have hedged me behind and before and laid your hand upon me." This is for our protection and help, *not* for judgment and condemnation. Psalm 103 says, "As a father has compassion on his child, so the Lord has compassion on those who fear Him; for He knows our frame. He remembers that we are dust." Think about it...*just how much can you expect from dust?*

Can you imagine receiving so much attention? It astounds me when I try to wrap my mind around this truth.

"Where can I go from Your Spirit, or where can I flee from Your presence? If I ascend into heaven, You are there; if I make my bed in hell behold, You are there."

I don't know about you, but I've made my bed in "hell on earth" more times than I care to recall. But Deuteronomy 33:27 says, "The eternal God is a dwelling place; and underneath are the everlasting arms." This is great news because we can never fall so low that His arms aren't there to catch us.

Let's pick up this great chapter in verse 13:

"...You have formed my inward parts, You knit me together in my mother's womb."

I really enjoy knitting. As I made a scarf one day, I realized that I touch every inch of yarn during the knitting process. By the time it's finished, I know every stitch and can identify it as my own work.

If you read the Genesis account of creation, you will discover that everything God made was spoken into existence by Him: God *said*, "let there be light;" God *said*, "let the earth bring forth grass...the living creature." But on the 6th day, He did things differently. He stooped down and picked up a handful of dirt and *formed* man. Then He breathed life into him. Later that day He made woman. Oh, not as an afterthought, but as His crowning achievement! You can almost hear the crescendo come to its peak as He proclaimed, "It is *very* good."

David continues in this psalm: "...I will praise You for I am fearfully and wonderfully made. Marvelous are Your works and that my soul knows very well." This could also be translated, "I am an awesome wonder." Only since the invention of the microscope have we been able to see the depths of this truth.

It also says every circumstance of our lives was written down – even before egg and sperm met.

As I look back on my life, there are many pages – chapters even – that I would tear out of that book if I could. Lots of things that I don't want recorded for all eternity are entered in those pages. The amazing thing is that God knew them before hand...and chose me anyway.

He also chose you!

Finally:

"...How precious are Your thoughts to me, O God! How great is the sum of them. If I should count them they would be more in number than the sand. *When I awake* I am still with You."

After reading this verse, someone took the time to count a measure of sand and discovered that 1 teaspoon contains approximately 5,000 grains. I took 2 cups of sand from the beach and you couldn't tell that I'd done so! Now imagine all the sand in the world...and when you wake up you are still with God! That's just ONE night's worth of thoughts!! He loves you so much that He can't take His eyes off you!

How privileged we are to be invited into a personal, vibrant, loving relationship with God Almighty!

"DRIVING" FAITH

It was a dark and moonless night. At 2 a.m. there wasn't much traffic on the freeway. As I peered into the dark watching for deer, I realized that night driving isn't much different than our Christian walk.

At night, the headlights illuminate just enough for us to see the next bend in the road. The darkness prevents us from seeing the "big" picture, but we can see a little way ahead and to the sides. The lines are important because they keep us on the road. Occasionally, without oncoming traffic, we can turn on the high beams. This permits a little more of our surroundings to be seen.

When we travel at night, it's important to avoid out-driving our headlights. Speeding, especially on mountain roads, can prove to be fatal. Storms and fog reduce our vision, requiring us to slow down...sometimes to a near standstill.

Isn't this like our walk with Christ? He illuminates our path just enough for us to see where we are headed next. We can barely see the curves in the road before us. The "big" picture is out there, but we lack the ability to see very much of it. In 1st Corinthians 13, we are told that for now we see as in a glass darkly. Occasionally He hits the "high beams," allowing us to see a little more of what He's doing around us.

If we are to travel with Christ and stay on the road it is *crucial* that we not go faster than God's illumination. If we're a little foggy about what to do next, it's a good time to slow down! Of course, the severity of the storm will determine whether we can continue at our normal pace, or slow down to improve our visibility. Some storms require us to stop all together until it lets up. I'm thankful for His perfect shelter in times like these!

Just as night driving requires vigilance if we're going to avoid unexpected obstacles, so our Christian walk requires vigilance for the same reason. We have an adversary who delights in putting obstacles in our paths, hoping that we're asleep at the wheel and will wreck!

On paved roads, we are given guidelines—the centerline and the fog line. On our path of life, we also have guidelines. The greatest commandment is that we love the Lord with all our heart, soul, mind, and strength. This is like the white sideline that keeps us on the road. The second—love your neighbor as yourself—is like the center line that keeps us out of another's lane, and from taking more than our share of the road, or causing them to crash!

Night driving takes a lot of faith. We've become so used to doing this that we don't think about it. Living the Christian life also requires a lot of faith. May we become so used to doing it that we don't have to think about it...just follow the Light and keep between the Lines!

DAVID AND GOLIATH

THERE ARE TWO INVALUABLE things that I learned from Chuck Missler. The first is the fact that every story in the Old Testament points to Christ (Psalm 40:7). The other is that when we find something we don't understand in the Bible, we should ask God to teach us – and then *expect* Him to do so.

My son, Rob, and I were recently looking at the story of David and Goliath to see how it pointed to Christ. We couldn't see it, so we asked God for insight.

Here's what we were shown:

It can be argued that David didn't kill Goliath. The stone killed him! David's job was to gather the stone, point it at Goliath, and release it to carry out its purpose.

In this story, we are "David." Our "Goliaths" are those things that would take us captive and destroy or kill us. Our "slingshots" are our prayers.

Jesus is the Rock. We need to appropriate Him, recognize His power to destroy our enemy, point Him at our Goliath, and release Him, by faith, to accomplish His purpose!

It's cool that David only used stones, not rocks. Is Jesus saying that it only takes a bit of His power to take down our enemies??

When a Goliath rears its ugly head in our lives, we need to, by faith, reckon him already dead. Then release the Lord, through prayer, to make it so!

If our faith is lacking, no problem! Ephesians 2:8 says that our faith is a gift. Ask the Lord to provide the faith you need in order to trust Him to bring down Goliath!

As you can see, even the story of David and Goliath *does* teach us something about Christ.

Try this for yourself. God delights in revealing Truth through His Word. Once you've found one of these for yourself, you'll be hooked!

PITCHED INSIDE AND OUT

GOD IS PLEASED WITH me. Why do I struggle with believing this? It is hard to accept when I see disapproval on so many of the faces around me. I discussed this with my son one morning.

You see, the Holy Spirit is inside us – given to us as a *seal* to prove that we belong to God. Furthermore, our position is in Christ. I told him this makes us like a sandwich – the Spirit within, Christ without.

Suddenly Noah's ark came into view. It was pitched inside and out. The interesting thing about the word for "pitch" is that everywhere else in the scriptures it is translated, "atonement!"

Work with me here…we live in tents – these are not our permanent homes. However, the insides of our tents are sealed with the Holy Spirit. The position of our tent is "in Christ." The ark becomes a sort of representation of us…sandwiched in between the two!

As we talked about this new revelation, I shared with my son how we can either be like the Sea of Galilee or the Dead Sea. We can bring life, prosperity, and refreshment to others by giving out what we have been given; or, we can only take in and never share thus becoming as dead as the Dead Sea!

This was certainly true in the above example. As I was giving out to my son what I knew about God, he was pouring new truth into me!

IN WHO'S NAME?

"IN JESUS' NAME, AMEN." Here's a phrase that we throw around, tacking it on whenever we feel it's appropriate. However, what does it mean?

Well, we've been given "power of attorney" to act on Christ's behalf, and in *His* best interest in His physical absence. In order to be carrying out His will, we *first need to know what His will is,* in any given situation.

For example, we arrived at the hospital and discovered that my mother had slipped into a coma. Although she was hooked up to a respirator, we all knew that *this was not her will.*

She told us countless times that she did not want to be kept alive by artificial means. She told us this when we walked, sat, stood, and laid down. We were well aware of her wishes.

A medical Power of Attorney had been issued beforehand, which assigned us the responsibility of carrying out her will should she become incapacitated. She was able to do so with assurance because she had taught her will to us. There was no hesitation in my dad, my brother, or I when we told the doctors to remove life support. We acted on her behalf – *in Gayle's name.* We were free of guilt as we did so. (Thanks, Mom!)

So it should be – and more so – with our Lord. We need His instruction continually so that we can truly act in His name.

Father, forgive me for the countless times I've taken Jesus' name in vain, slapping it on prayers that were my will...and not His. Help me to know His will so that I can speak and act on His behalf…a worthy executor of His Power of Attorney.

This prayer <u>is</u>…"in Jesus' Name," Amen!

- 3 -

Lessons In Time

"A HUNDRED YEARS FROM NOW..."

"A HUNDRED YEARS FROM now will this matter?" I'm always amazed at how many situations are quickly brought into perspective for me when I ask this.

When I first came across this question in the 80's, I tried it out on the problems I was dealing with at the time. Every one of them is a non-issue today. In fact, only one or two continued to be a problem at the end of the year. There was the mailbox I was terrified of opening because it was full of bills I couldn't pay; the empty cupboards, fridge and freezer with only pictures of food taped in them; the Class IV Pap smear; the struggles at work...these were all resolved long ago. They came and went...and God was faithful through it all.

One by one I picked up "anchors" from Scripture that steadied me when the winds of adversity blew. It seems like many of us are facing trials and struggles right now, so I thought I'd share them with you.

The first one I picked up is Romans 8:28. If you don't know another verse in the Bible, you *have* to memorize this one. It's worth its weight in gold. It says, "and we know God causes all things to work together for good to those who love

God..." This was the only promise I had to cling to for a long time. As I looked at my life, I wondered how God was going to pull it off. I'm happy to report that He has!

The second scripture I picked up several years later. It gives me added stability during life's storms. It is Jeremiah 29:11, and says, "'I know the plans I have for you,' declares the Lord, 'plans for good and not for evil, to give you a future and a hope.'"

Plans for good and not for evil...I need that reminder as much today as I did when we were staying at the Women's Refuge.

The third scripture is especially dear to me because sometimes I fall. In the past, I've found myself in some incredibly deep pits. But, "The eternal God is your refuge; and underneath are the everlasting arms." (Deuteronomy 33:27) This is a true word. We can never fall so low that He won't be there to catch us and lift us up once again.

The last Scripture is one that I claimed as my own just before my mom moved to heaven. Second Corinthians 4:17-18 says, "For our *light* affliction, which is but for a *moment*, is working for us a far more exceeding and eternal weight of glory, while we do not look at the things which are seen, but at the things which are not seen. For the things which are seen are temporary, but the things which are not seen are eternal." These trials and tribulations are *not* going to last forever. This Scripture will breathe hope into any difficulty!

May I encourage you to write these down on 3 x 5 cards? Post them around your house, put a copy into your purse or wallet, and memorize them. Then when you are feeling overwhelmed, begin speaking them, personalize them and pray them back to God, sing them, whisper them, shout them to the heavens! They will help keep the focus on our Lord who is our strength and our high tower. They will give us feet like hinds' feet and set us on our high places. (Psalm 18:33)

THIS IS THE DAY

THIS IS THE DAY. *This* is the day. *This* is the day that the Lord has made. The heavenly Father is a God of economy. He does not create space maintainers. He is the very God whom Paul claimed makes *all* things work together for good. *All* things.

Do we spend many days in succession waiting for that glorious day when everything will be perfect – and *then* we will be happy? Oh, how happy we will be on that day, we believe!

No, no, a thousand times, no! *This* is the day that the Lord has made. We will rejoice and be glad in *it.*

Every time we say, "Today I can't be happy because of such-and-so," we throw away the precious moments of our lives. For some of us, it isn't just moments, it is entire hours, days, months, or even years. *Tomorrow* things will be better and then I can be happy.

Perhaps it's time to get a different perspective of our lives.

Do yourself a favor. The next time you get so bogged down that you can't wait for tomorrow, take a walk. Look around at your world. *Really* look at the trees. Watch the birds. Smell the flowers. There is *always* something to rejoice and be glad in. Always. Oh, sure, sometimes it doesn't hit you the moment you step out the door. It will probably take a lot of effort on your part; but it's worth it.

Take your eyes off the battle you're fighting. Focus on something else for a little bit. For heaven's sake, *lighten up!*

"Pile up a lot of tomorrows and you'll find yourself with a heap of unlived yesterdays!" (From *The Music Man*)

This is not criticism from an outsider who doesn't understand. Even as I write, I am dealing with one of the most difficult and heated battles of my entire life. Nevertheless, the need for a new perspective was pointed out to me by a very dear, caring Friend. He let me know that He'd made *this* day, as well as every other, and that there are good things for me to enjoy even now. Not when things get better, but *today*.

So. What will it be? Will we waste today while we dream of tomorrow, or will we take this opportunity to live today to the fullest? Hmm, come to think of it, I'm long overdue for that walk in the garden!

LIFE IS JUST AROUND THE CORNER

I DON'T KNOW ABOUT you, but my ship still hasn't come in. There's always something better around the corner for which I live in anticipation, casting aside today's gifts as insignificant.

In four years, my youngest son will have graduated from high school and I won't have to focus on teaching him anymore. *Then* I'm really going to begin living. I'll finally have time to learn how to play the piano. I'll get back to playing my clarinet and sax. The songs in my head will finally make it to paper – and hopefully to our congregation. I'll write that book which I know the whole world is just dying to read.

When my marriage becomes perfect, I'll be so content. It will be the sort of relationship that has the world banging on our door because they want to discover our secret. I just know they will!

My yard will no longer look like an overgrown jungle, but will become the Garden of Eden that I just know it can be. My neighbors will love me because, for the first time since we moved here, we will look like everyone else.

My children will all realize how much they need Jesus and come to Him. Then our relationships will be healed and we will love each other perfectly. Ah! That will be the day. My life will be fulfilled then.

God has something really big planned for me and it's just ahead. I know it! Haven't you all been told, "God has a wonderful plan for your life"? I'm waiting...I've been waiting for nearly 40 years – since the first time I heard that. I wanted to believe it with all my heart. There absolutely had to be something better than what I was living at the time!

Suddenly it dawned on me – this *is* His plan for me *right now*. He desires that I teach our son. He has lessons for me in that – perseverance, dependence on Him, obedience, sacrificial giving, and many more.

My marriage can't be perfect because I am not yet perfect myself – and my husband is God's favorite tool to fashion me into the woman He desires me to be! (A side note on this topic: – the world teaches us that marriage is about romance and happiness. However, God is infinitely more interested in our holiness than our happiness. Once realized, this gave me a very different outlook on my own relationship. My dear husband brings out the worst in me – and he's meant to, so that God can deal with my stuff! Knowing this helps me work with God, instead of against Him.)

My yard…it's a yard, for goodness sake! If I don't fit into the neighborhood – well, I wasn't meant to.

A wonderful scripture reads, "*this* is the day that the Lord has made, let us *rejoice* and be glad in it." (Psalm 118:24) We are commanded – yes commanded – to rejoice repeatedly in the Bible. Is life passing us by? Do we miss feeling fulfilled today because things will be better tomorrow? Tomorrow may never come. We will have died waiting for our ship to come in – whatever that may mean to us.

Oswald Chambers reminds us well: "God is not working toward a particular finish -- His purpose with me is in the process itself. The process, not the outcome, is glorifying to God." In Philippians 4:11 Paul encourages us to learn to be content in whatsoever state we are in, whether we have a lot or a little, are hated or loved. In Philippians 4:4 he tells us, "Rejoice in the Lord always."

It's time for me to quit living in the future, and to enjoy the present. As I write this I realize that I'm living yesterday's "tomorrow" and it's nothing like what I had anticipated! Either I missed the boat entirely, or was suckered into believing a lie and wasted precious days waiting for "someday" to come.

We live in a fallen world. Remember that. Our lives just aren't going to be perfect this side of heaven. Let's stop living in tomorrow, and rejoice for all we have today. Tomorrow will take care of itself.

WHERE CAN I GO?

CHILDREN ARE AMAZING examples of the truths in Your Word.

For instance, I watched my friends' little girl during the day for one month. She was a cute little four-year-old.

It had been a while since I'd hung out with a little kid on a daily basis, so it was disconcerting to have her follow me everywhere. If I went outside, she followed me; if I would go to the garage and turn around – there she was! Even opening the bathroom door quickly would cause her to fall into the room!

Suddenly I saw it! "Where can I go from Your Spirit; and where can I flee from Your presence?" David wrote in Psalm 139. You are with me like that – stuck to me like glue. Oh, that I would be as acutely aware of You, as I was of that dear little child!

THE GRAND ILLUSION

SEVERAL YEARS AGO, WE attended a "special meeting" being held at a church. Their drawing card was an illusionist/evangelist. He used sleight-of-hand to share the gospel. He was very good.

Toward the end of his presentation, he drew a complicated diagram to show how God has a plan for our lives; but when we make bad choices, we miss out on His "best" plan, and get relegated to plan B or C. Not knowing any better, I swallowed this hook, line, and sinker. By this guy's reckoning, I'm probably on Plan ABZ – having made so many choices that were not God's will for me!

Do you feel this way? I don't know about you, but I've wasted countless hours playing the "if only" game. It goes like this: Things would have been so much different, so much better, "if only" I'd _____ (fill in the blank).

For fun yesterday, I began with a single "if only." "If only my parents hadn't divorced." I could give you several pages of things that would be completely different about me – I'm serious. I realized, after I followed just one "if only" to its conclusion, that I would be a totally different person. I would be living in a completely different state – and not who I am at all today.

For the first time, I realized that I didn't miss the "best" road for me. It doesn't exist. It's merely a figment of my imagination. It's an illusion, created by an adversary that wants me to believe that I'm getting a "2nd-best" kind of life. With my enemy's help, I've wasted a lot of time replaying and regretting the choices that I've made, which robs me of the joy of the gift that I have in today.

Now I understand why Paul said, "forgetting those things which are behind and reaching forward to those things which are ahead, I press toward the goal for the prize of the upward call of God in Christ Jesus." (Philippians 3:13,14) Today I see the great wisdom in that. My choices were part of God's plan for my life – factored in before I was born.

Psalm 139:16 reads, "...And in Your book they all were written, the days fashioned for me, when as yet there were none of them." He didn't have to develop a "workaround" for my screw-ups. He knew them all in advance and designed my life accordingly. God is omniscient (a fancy word that means "knows everything); and this was all taken into account before the foundations of the world.

This is good news for all of us. As we look back over our lives and the mistakes we've made, we need to remember that they have brought us to this place. We don't have to wonder what would have happened "if..." Everything that we've been through, every choice we've made was all figured into the Master Plan.

What an amazing God we serve! What a great privilege to be called by His name. I'm sure we don't even know the half of it.

It's time for us to put away our dreams of what life would have been – could have been – "if only." "If" I would have gone away to college; "if" I would have moved to another state when I had the chance; "if" I would have made any of those other choices I could have, then I wouldn't have my husband, my children, or this great fellowship...and I wouldn't know you!

What contentment we have when we realize that we are right where God knew we would be at this time in our lives.

Lord, how thankful I am that You are sovereign, all-knowing and in control, no matter what "wrong" turns we've taken. They've all led us to this place, at this time. Thank You for the knowledge that we are right on track and progressing according to Your plan. Thank You, also, for the things we've learned along the way – both from our good choices and our bad ones. These choices have made us who we are today.

In Jesus' Name

– Amen

TO CHOOSE OR NOT TO CHOOSE

ROMANS 11:29 READS, "God's gifts and calling are irrevocable." He offers us gifts, and He has a calling for us. The question is this: are we going to accept them?

For instance, take the calling that He has for us. We can choose to accept it, we can decline it, or we can choose not to choose – to let someone else choose for us.

The last one has been my choice for many years. God has called me to a specific ministry. I didn't choose to accept it...but I didn't decline it either. I've left it up to others to decide for me. How silly is that?

For most of my adult life, I have been waiting to be given "permission" to enter into my calling (I guess God's permission wasn't good enough!). Perhaps it is because I wasn't convinced that He was calling me. I wanted it confirmed by people "in the know" about such things. If they didn't see it, then I must be imagining things.

The problem was that I didn't give them anything to see! How could they possibly know if these were my calling or my gifts if I never actually used them? It would have taken an Old Testament prophet to be able to see into my future and say, "Yes, dear, that is what I see you doing in the 21st century." Have you seen one of them around lately? No? Neither have I!

I have waited and waited and waited for that "right" person to grant permission for me to step into what I believe God has called me to do. I'm still waiting, and I'm pretty sure I will be waiting until the day I die if I don't decide to act on what I believe I am supposed to be doing!

Lately I've been paying close attention to my "rule book." As it turns out, I have quite a few rules by which I live my life and on which I base my decisions. One of the rules in my book states, "You shall not do anything without a divine word from a reliable prophet." Since these "words" are few and far between, I haven't done much, as you might have guessed!

Where I got this "rule book" from, I have no idea. Well, I have a strong suspicion. Most likely, it came from an enemy who wants to leave me sitting on the bench, watching life go by. His plan is to keep me from entering the game.

At this rate, at the end of my life I'll be whining that I never had an opportunity to do something for God. The opportunity has been there all along...I've just been waiting for the right permission from the right source – whoever *that* might be.

It's time to begin making choices for myself. It's time to quit delegating this task to people who, with less-than-pure motives, will probably withhold the coveted approval. I sat by and let others tell me what I was supposed to be doing with my life for just about long enough. That's what I've done, you know, cowered on the bench and let life go on without me, all the while wishing I could be a part of it. Enough!!!

Father, a life lived in fear is a life half-lived. I want to begin living the abundant life You speak of in Your Word. I repent of my lack of faith that You will guide me every day, in all things great or small (Proverbs 3:5,6). Help me to live a life that glorifies You as I walk in Your strength and Your power.

In Jesus' Name,

Amen.

CLEANSING THE WOUNDS

A SPLINTER LEFT TO itself will eventually fester. Once the pressure becomes great enough it will erupt – ejecting the foreign object. While it remains in the body, it causes infection. If it gets serious enough it can cause grave illness and even death. If the blood becomes involved, the life-sustaining fluid, it begins to clot, shutting down vital organs as it goes throughout the body.

I know this because it happened to my mother. The result was death...from three little kidney stones.

An interesting analogy can be drawn from this example, but it takes place in the heart where no known medical tests can diagnose it.

The arrows we've received from the adversary are foreign bodies in our hearts. Left there, resentment begins. Bitterness follows, or it becomes a sense of worthlessness, fear, hopelessness, etc. These infectious emotions begin to circulate until every fiber of our being is involved, choking off our very life. The various "organs" in our heart cease to function properly. The filters don't sort out truth and lies. Nothing gets "digested" properly and we become immobilized – just the way the enemy likes us!

However, when we go to the Great Physician, Jehovah Rapha, and submit to Him, He cleans out our wounds. As He applies the balm of Gilead, we find new life.

When I first wrote this, I submitted myself to the healing of many old wounds. Although this may sound silly, I listed them on paper. Then I purchased two helium-filled balloons. My lists were written on them. When this was done, I prayed over each item, forgiving the offender or asking forgiveness for myself. The lists were burned as I wrote. Later that day I took my balloons and released them to the Lord for Him to take care of according to His good purpose. He was the only one who could heal me.

In the past, I've dealt with wounds in various ways. Once they're given to God healing begins. Sometimes it's instantaneous, but more often it takes a period of time...not unlike a physical illness would.

I like doing something symbolic because it provides a "stone of remembrance" for me to point to when the adversary brings it up again.

God's glory is revealed in a woman fully alive.

Please restore my soul.

- 4 -

Lessons Of Life

BE STILL

AS THE PLANE TOOK off, I was so tired that I could barely keep my eyes open. All of my plans for a great time of studying the Word during my flight were left on the ground. Therefore, I slept.

If you look at the picture taken of me by the DMV just the week before my vacation, and then look at pictures taken only a few days into it, you would notice a great difference. In the first one, I look like I haven't slept in months. In the second photo, I look quite rested and calm.

What made the difference? During those first few days, while everyone was out of the house, I was still before God.

Being still is not a strong point for me. It probably isn't yours, either – not in a production-driven world. We think we have to be doing something of significance every second of every day. If not, we're taking up space and valuable resources on our planet and ought to move over and make room for someone who is going to do something useful.

However, God calls for us to be still. He tells us that when we wait upon Him we will renew our strength. He says, "Come unto Me, all you who labor and are heavy laden and I will give you rest." He invites each of us to take one day a week and focus on what is truly important...our relationship with Him. Will we do it? How can we possibly, with so many things needing our attention?

Something I noticed a couple of years ago, though, was that I was spending a lot of time complaining to the Lord about the amount and quality of time that I had with my husband. We were in a tough spot in our relationship, so we were mostly avoiding each other.

As I was whining to Him about it (I'm a good whiner!), I sensed Him asking why I was so dissatisfied with the state of my marital relationship. The Lord gently pointed out that, unless it was to complain to Him about my life, I really wasn't talking to Him. In fact, I was so busy griping that He had been unable to get a word in edgewise! Once I'd said my piece the conversation was over and I'd go on my way. Come to think of it, it wasn't much of a conversation; rather, it was a monologue.

It's beginning to be apparent that many of the problems I experience in my marriage are mere reflections of my relationship with God. He seems to use people around me to show me how He feels about the way I am either treating or neglecting Him.

"Be still, and know that I am God." Short, sweet, simple – so simple. Our little human minds say, "too simple!"

I have to DO something, like the little pink bunny that keeps on going and going! For all of our superior intelligence we forget that we are called "human Beings," and *not* "human Doings." What are we really called to do?

"He has told you, oh (wo)man, what is good and what the Lord requires of you, but to do justly and to love mercy and to walk humbly with your God." (Micah 6:8)

JUST CLAY

WE ARE MADE OF clay – *clay*! There is *nothing* good in us apart from Christ. Oh, that we would grasp the true meaning of this.

Without God, we are *nothing*. Unless *He* adds the necessary nutrients, does the sowing, the tending, nothing in us is good. Nothing we do on our own, in ourselves or in others, will amount to anything.

The yard surrounding my home is clay. Red clay. It stains everything it touches. We are like that. Whatever we try to do in our own "natural" state is no different. Look at the lives we've "stained" when we've tried to make things happen in our own strength.

Clay has horrible properties. Under heat, it becomes hard and brittle. An abundance of water causes it to turn to slime. Isn't this just like us? When the trials come, if we try to get through them on our own, we become hard and embittered. When abundance comes our way (through prosperity, education, etc.), if we are not submitted to the Lord, we will become just so much slime – arrogant, proud, and self-centered.

It is no wonder that the Lord has to allow our hearts to be plowed up so He can work His Holy Spirit into us. Without Him, we have very little worth. The lush garden of Psalm 1:3 will only be a dream without tilling the soil of our hearts and working in the necessary ingredients to make us rich. (*He is like a tree planted by streams of water, which yields its fruit in season and whose leaf does not wither. Whatever he does prospers)*

And we are rich when we submit ourselves to the Lord and allow him to do His heavy work within us. It is only through the hard work of overturning the soil of our hearts that we can begin to bear the fruit of the Spirit – love, joy, peace, longsuffering, etc. (Galatians 5:22,23) It is only when we submit to His preparations within us that we will become fertile.

Once the groundwork is done, the weather around us will be of little consequence. Our garden will flourish whether it is hot or cold, wet or dry. Our circumstances will have little effect on the fruit we bear. Being prosperous by worldly standards will not be so important. Being popular will not matter because the Lord Himself will be the one who walks through our garden and takes pleasure in the work of His hands. Lightening strikes will only add to the beauty there (ever seen a Japanese Bonsai?). Fire will add to the fertility of our soil.

If you desire, He will allow you to take over the tending of your private garden. Be aware, however, that it will soon return to clay. The plants will shrivel and cease to bear fruit. Our first state will be worse than the first, for we will have seen the beauty that the Holy Spirit can create when we allow *Him* to be the Gardener. We will mourn the loss of the beauty within us with immeasurable grief.

But when we confess our sins, He is faithful and just to forgive us our sins, and to cleanse us from all unrighteousness (1 John 1:9). Take comfort from these words. Take advantage of them. Let God be the Gardener of your heart, transforming your clay into a thing of beauty.

HOW LOW CAN WE GO?

SOLOMON WAS BORN TO David and Bathsheba. Yep, *that* Bathsheba. Think about the implications of this truth.

When David and Bathsheba met, both were married – to someone else. Was she a willing participant in the affair or did she feel trapped into obeying the king? Scripture is vague, and I've heard arguments for both sides. Either way, a consequence was that she became pregnant.

Have you ever noticed how unconfessed sin seems to snowball? It certainly did for David. Coveting and lust led to adultery. Bathsheba's pregnancy led him into manipulation and murder. Romans 6:23 states, "...the wages of sin is death..." When we sin, something dies. It will not necessarily be the immediate physical death of a person, but may instead be relationships, our integrity, our character, or our witness.

David was a godly man, filled with the Holy Spirit. Something went terribly wrong though. When he finally came to his senses, the depths to which he had fallen must have devastated him.

Many of us have found ourselves doing things that we would never have believed we were capable of. For some, this meant a bout with alcohol or drugs. For others, it may have been an affair. It may have been overspending or overeating...this page could be filled with endless possibilities and still have more to list! One thing led to another and another—until there we were, beaten down and hoping that we wouldn't run into any of our old church friends.

David knew something, though. It is great news for those of us who have fallen at some point. In Psalm 103:11,12 he penned these words: "For as the heavens are high above the earth, so great is His mercy toward those who fear Him; as far as the east is from the west, so far has He removed our transgressions from us."

What saddens my heart is that although we've confessed our sin, we live as though we were second-class citizens of heaven. We feel that we no longer have the privilege of aspiring to be used mightily of God. We believe we blew it so badly that our value to the body of believers has been lost forever. Is this true?

Fast-forward to the end of David's life. All of his wives (except Michal) bore him children. However, which one gave birth to the child that *God* chose to succeed David? Bathsheba; *she* is in the lineage of Jesus!!

In this story, recorded for our learning, we find proof of God's total pardon when confession is made!!! It is a beautiful example of just how freely and completely we are forgiven!

Thank You, Jesus, for bearing our shame so that we could be dressed in robes of righteousness. Thank You for recording the lives of David and Bathsheba so we could know how thoroughly You forgive us.

NO LOWLIFE CHRISTIANS

RAISING SEVEN CHILDREN WILL give you a perspective on God's love for His children like nothing else I could imagine. Perhaps not when they're little and making you crazy, but once they've grown and you stroll down Memory Lane.

No two of them were exactly alike. Nor were there two who ever came close to the others in personality, characteristics, or behavior. Each of them had their good points and their not-so-good points! Some were more obedient, some were more loving, some were more considerate, etc. Did we have any favorites? You bet your life! Christian was a favorite because he was the first, and showed us the wonders of being a parent. Beth was a favorite because she was second, and she showed us the wonders of being a parent. Charity was a favorite because she was third, and she showed us the wonders of being a parent! The same is true of my fourth – Tyree; fifth – Drew; sixth – Ted; and seventh – Rob! In their own way, each of them is a favorite. That's because they are different.

As I type, I wonder what it would have been like to raise six carbon copies of Christian. One of him is awesome. Six more just like him and I'd have been ready for the loony bin! Six more just like *any* of them would have the same effect, I think!

One thing I know about my kids, though, is that each of them secretly envies at least one sibling's personality or a characteristic they possess. They look at one another and think somehow they missed out by not being...whatever it is they think would make them a better person or more lovable.

"Oh, if only I were like So and So. *Then* I would be worth something." Have you ever thought this? I know that my kids are not alone in their thoughts. I've done it myself — countless times.

Apparently, this was a problem in the Corinthian church as well. Otherwise, Paul would never have written the section that we find in 1 Corinthian 12. It reads: *"If the foot should say, 'Because I am not a hand, I am not of the body,' is it therefore not of the body? And if the ear should say, 'Because I am not an eye, I am not of the body,' is it therefore not of the body?"*

What on earth would cause him to write such a thing? Were they comparing themselves to one another — seemingly coming up on the short end of the stick?

Did the teachers want to be like the worship leaders; the worship leaders like the greeters; the greeters like the pastors? Were they assessing greater value to certain gifts and lesser value to others? It would seem so.

Yet, I have to tell you that although we don't necessarily want to "parade" certain body parts — it would not be proper — neither would we want to make do without them! Face it; those "unseemly" parts are absolutely vital to our health and well-being! Even the one we use as a cuss word...you know the one! Sew that baby shut and see how you hold up. Within a week, you'll be in the hospital — dying!

In 2 Corinthians 10:12 Paul says, "For we dare not class ourselves or compare ourselves with those who commend themselves. But they, measuring themselves by themselves, and comparing themselves among themselves *are not wise."* (Emphasis mine)

The minute we begin comparing ourselves to anyone else, according to this verse, we are not being wise. We will always find someone "better" than we are...at least in our own eyes. We will come up lacking, and go away depressed. Or, we will applaud ourselves for not being "as bad" as they are, and go away quite proud of ourselves.

In the comparison game, there has to be a winner and a loser. That's the purpose of comparing. Which one is better? Which one is worse? Once in a while, they might be the same – but not when it comes to people. We're all unique, so we will have different characteristics in differing amounts.

To be sure, this is where we get ourselves into trouble. Once comparisons begin, one thing is certain: pride has reared its ugly head! Why else would we want to compare ourselves to someone else? Every time, we will either come out as "superior" to them, or walk away feeling like we don't measure up. Pride. How do I know? I know because comparison makes it all about *us*, and not all about *Jesus*.

Think of how many more people we would like – even love – if we were to stop making comparisons. Think of the conflicts that would cease if envy were to be evicted from our thoughts. Imagine the freedom that comes with being OK with who we are – whatever our packaging may be, or any of the other things that make us uniquely us!

We are exactly who God wants us to be; perfectly equipped for the work He has planned for us. Besides, if we're busy giving our best impression of someone else, then *who will be us?* The world needs our personal contribution, our unique combination of skills, talents, appearance, and personalities. Without a doubt God, who knows everything, considered for a brief moment what it would be like to deal with 6 billion people just like me and said, "No, thanks!" Don't laugh. He thought about 6 billion people just like you and said the same thing!

A friend of mine, Jake, put 1 Corinthians 12:18 in a nutshell. His comment, although meant to be humorous, was more profound than I think he realized. He said, "There are no low-life Christians." I don't think I've ever heard it put better!

Now and again, the realization that I am exactly who God knew I would be at this moment in time – with all my blunders and struggles – washes over me like I'm hearing it for the first time. Suddenly, I feel clean and light. The heaviness I've been packing around slips from my shoulders...

...once again I remember that I am free to be the person Jesus created!

DO I WANT TO BE MADE WELL?

WE WERE AT A birthday party when a woman suddenly cried out in pain. She had been playing on the floor with the kids, and her hip dislocated when she tried to get back into the chair.

Present at the party, were two young healing ministry students. I saw volumes communicated as they excitedly looked at one another. "Here's our chance!"

They went over to the woman and asked if they could pray for her. She agreed. Following their prayer, they commanded her to rise and be healed. I cringed. She tried to stand up, but it was to no avail. Nothing had changed.

Now, let me tell you that I believe God *can* and *does* heal instantly today. I've been the recipient of two miraculous healings myself. But I knew something that they apparently didn't. They forgot to ask a very important question: "Do you *want* to be made well?"

As strange as it may sound, there are many people today who, deep down, really don't want to be free of their affliction. In our society, there are a lot of perks to being disabled. Among them are a disability check, freedom from holding down a job, drugs to keep them anesthetized, pity from others, and a lot of attention. Although she didn't like the pain, she was not ready to give up the benefits she received from her disability.

There are also people today who have been praying freedom over a spouse who is hooked on alcohol, drugs, or stuck in other bondages; but in their heart of hearts, they don't really want change. There are perks to being married to an alcoholic, or having problem children. They make us look good. Their over-the-top bad behavior makes our "little" behavioral issues seem reasonable.

You see there have been things in my own life that I've prayed for, year after year. Nothing had changed, though. There were prayers for freedom from bondages for myself, prayers for a united marriage, prayers for intimacy with God. Every one of these, I knew, was a prayer according to God's will. There was no scriptural reason why He should not be acting on them...or was there?

Stay with me. I hope that this will illuminate a possible reason for unanswered prayer. It certainly has for me!

At the Pool of Bethesda Jesus encountered a man who had an infirmity thirty-eight years. When Jesus saw him lying there, and knew that he already had been in that condition a long time, He said to him, *"Do you want to be made well?"* (John 5:5,6)

We expect to hear an enthusiastic, "YES!" Instead, he gives excuses for his continued infirmity. He tells why he can't get to the water in time; how he has no one to help him in, how the others get there first.

Jesus said, "Rise, take up your bed and walk." (John 5:8). At this point, the fellow has choices to make. Will he continue to offer excuses and stay there? Will he say, "Well, OK, tomorrow I'll try that"? I want to cheer for him as he makes the choice to get up and go on his way!!

It took a lot of courage for him to get up. This had become a lifestyle for him. Remember, he had suffered with this infirmity for *thirty-eight* years. Once he stood up, it would be to a whole new life; full of responsibilities he would have to take on once again...or maybe for the first time.

On a personal note, however, there was a time in my past when I spent hours and hours praying for a man. He was a truly unpleasant fellow, outrageous in his behavior, who believed it was his job to cut everyone down to size. To say that he was difficult to live with is an understatement.

Looking back I can see that while part of me really did want him to be set free, there was a secret part of my heart that didn't want things to change. Does that sound crazy? Well, think about it. His outrageous behavior was an excellent cover for my own. He was my excuse for tirades and all sorts of bad behavior. Besides, if he changed I was going to have to forgive him for all the ways he had hurt the children and me.

The idea that God would touch him and completely heal him terrified me. I would have to give up my right to hate him (not that I had a right in the first place), and I would have to straighten up myself. My plans for life without him would have to be scrapped. I wasn't prepared to do that. "Enough was enough," I thought, and now it was time for me to move on, regardless of what God did.

God calls this a divided heart. In James 1:6, 7 it says, "But let him ask in faith with no doubting, for he who doubts is like a wave of the sea driven and tossed by the wind. For let not that man suppose that he will receive anything from the Lord; he is a *double-minded* man, unstable in all his ways."

This described me perfectly. The "doubt" herein described is not a fleeting uncertainty, but a division of allegiance. I wanted God's will of a healed marriage on one hand, but I wanted my will to be done, on the other.

Those of us with lousy marriages are often divided in our desire, but not consciously. In part, we want them to live fully for the Lord. However, we secretly enjoy our "one-upness." We're "better" than they are, and we "know" it. If they become transformed, we suddenly are unveiled for the Pharisees we really are.

Maybe this is why God took His time answering my requests concerning my marriage, husband, and children. To be totally, painfully honest, I enjoyed being the more "righteous" one. People admired me when I kept sticking it out against the odds. I seemed so spiritual when I prayed for my poor "unenlightened" ones. People paid attention to me, showed concern for me, and pitied me. Would I lose their care if we finally got it all together? It was scary to think of giving all of that up; but I did.

There have been many times in my life where, in retrospect, I find this to be true. I genuinely wanted freedom for the person I was praying for; but I genuinely (secretly) hoped they would not change.

As I look around me, I realize that I am not alone in this double-mindedness. It is very common for an alcoholic to be dumped by the very people who demanded that he quit drinking. He sobers up only to find himself alone. His wife wanted him sober (she thought), but discovered that she no longer had his bad behavior behind which to hide her own. She would now have to take responsibility for her words and actions. She would have to forgive, and begin to love again. She would have to learn to live life without the daily adrenaline rush she was used to living with.

Most of the time, though, she leaves and finds another addicted person so life can go back to her concept of "normal."

My prayer is that God would show me where my allegiances are divided, and that He will bridge the chasm of my double-minded heart. It takes a lot of energy to live with a divided heart, jumping from one view (Lord, please heal...) to the other (I don't care what You do, Lord, I've had it!). This type of seesaw thinking makes a person incredibly unstable. It's hard to know what to expect from them minute by minute!

   Father, it is my earnest desire to be more like You. I cannot do this if I remain double-minded. Please heal any gaps in my heart so that I can be effective in praying for others. Above all, make me well!

- 5 -

Lessons In Marriage

THE CROSS

WHAT A BEAUTIFUL PICTURE of relationships the cross provides. The comparative length of each piece is significant. The upright beam represents our relationship to Christ, while the crossbeam our relationships with one another.

As important as relationships are for us, our relationship with Christ is of greater importance. Thus, the upright beam is longer than the horizontal one.

Without the upright beam, which represents our relationship with Jesus, there is nothing to support or hold up our relationships – especially our marriages. When we have a relationship with Christ, our life on the horizontal is elevated and we no longer have to lie in the dirt of the world.

The crossbeam of the cross represents our human relationships. The phrase "so heavenly conscious you're no earthly good" is the hallmark of a life with no crossbeam, only the upright. It is a life with no width...a life that does not affect others. An example of this is the "under-cover Christian." When we live secretly as believers, we are ignoring the directive to "let your light so shine before men...."

To omit either the upright beam (our relationship with God) or crossbeam (our relationships with others) is to lose the picture of the cross. All that is seen by the world is a stick in the dirt or a board on the ground!

The cross was set into the ground to show the depths to which Christ was willing to go to elevate us. In our relationships, let's "go ye therefore and do likewise."

HISTORY REPEATS

History had never been my favorite subject – unless it was to ridicule those who have repeated the same mistakes over and over again. As far as I was concerned, the only real reason to study history was to give me someone to feel superior to.

However, I was asked recently if I'd ever had an experience that drove me to my knees. The answer is "yes," several times! Uh, oh!

Having repented from putting down those who do not learn from their mistakes, I've decided to tell you about it.

As a bright-eyed 18 year old I knew one thing...I needed a savior. Oh, not the "Jesus" Savior. I already had Him. Rather I believed that I needed a flesh-and-blood one. I shopped at the local Bible College and found one that I believed would fit the bill.

We were married just a couple of months later. It took less than a week to discover that my husband had many "flaws" (at least, in *my* eyes), and was not my idea of a savior at all. As disillusionment set in and I became less-than-ladylike, we spent less and less time together. Sadly, our marriage lasted about 18 months.

Pregnant & *desperate* for a "savior," certain that no one would want my child or me, I accepted the first one to offer. For 10 years, I tried to mold him into the "savior" that I knew he could be if he would just try. As for problems, history repeated itself – only to a much greater degree this time.

This time I reached out for my true Savior who immediately began setting me free. The next couple of years would be the closest I'd ever been to Him. He spoke to me daily through my Bible – guiding me step by step. It was amazing!

Nevertheless, history does repeat itself. This time, instead of at a Bible college, I went shopping at the bars. Oh, not drinking. I liked to dance, and you can't drink and dance very well at the same time. I met a man who introduced me to a man. In no time, I was back to looking for a flesh-and-blood savior. Now, with 4 children in tow, I didn't figure I could be too picky.

From that relationship (which also lasted about 18 months), I found myself with a new, sure to be perfect "savior." Since I now had 6 kids, I thought myself lucky when he asked me to marry him.

It took no time at all for him to crumble under the weight of "saviorhood" and to back far away from me!

Not realizing that the problem was my neediness, I began to blame myself for being a no-good bum: worthless, and hopeless.

When things once again spiraled way out of control, I went back to my true Savior. Once again, He picked me up, brushed me off, and began leading me. Because of the many hurts I'd incurred by this time (and blaming God for all of them – after all He *could* have kept me from being hurt if He had wanted to), I was not so quick to run to His arms and to trust Him as fully as I had the last time. It's taken much longer (nearly a decade) for Him to make His way into my heart and begin healing me.

The thing is, history repeated itself. I just didn't see it at the time. I thought I was just going to have to work extra hard to find someone who was "nearly Christ-like" when it came to love. I went through husbands like a woman selecting a ripe cantaloupe – discarding those that were not sweet enough! What a mockery I made of the marriage vows. Needless to say, I'm not so quick to ridicule anyone for repeating mistakes anymore!

The thing that amazes me most in this is the patience and longsuffering of our Lord. He waited for many years, watching me destroy every commandment, picking up this idol and that one. He waited, seeing the pain I was inflicting on others, as I struggled so hard to find fulfillment in humans. Still He waited.

Once He had my attention again, He began patiently renewing my mind, helping me to sort through the Truth and the lies. It has been a slow and tedious process, but He has been merciful and gracious. Never once has He chided me for not "getting it." He doesn't tear me down for the mess I've made of things; He just keeps loving me and loving me. Slowly, He has been winning access to the deep recesses where I allow no one to go. He's good like that!

What astounds me is that, as with the Israelites, God has not "squished" me for my attempts to make people into idols, or for worshipping them as if they were a type of god.

Looking back, I know exactly why things haven't worked out. The Bible says, "I am God, that is My Name, and I will not give my glory to another, nor My praise to graven images." I had elevated man to the status of god, and He was not having any part of it! When things got bad enough it finally drove me to my knees and back to the One True God. Today, so long as I remember Who is God- and who is not – things run fairly smooth. The minute I begin trying to substitute my marriage for my relationship with God, things begin to go south once again.

Acts 3:19-20 says, "Repent therefore and be converted, that your sins may be blotted out, so that times of refreshing may come from the presence of the Lord, and that He may send Jesus Christ, who was preached to you."

Does my history resemble your own? Have you also repeated mistakes as you've tried to find someone or something else to fill the place in your heart that belongs only to God? He is a jealous God and desires that you be His, first and foremost.

THE KING'S HEART

THE KING'S HEART IS in the hand of the Lord, like the rivers of water, He turns it wherever He wishes. (Proverbs 21:1)

I wonder how many of us believed we had found "God in human skin" when we got married. This person met our needs like no one we had previously known, they met needs we didn't even realize we had! This was our opportunity to live happily ever after. It seemed too good to be true...

...and it was! Oh, some get to live the fantasy for a year or two. Others aren't so fortunate and reality sets in pretty quickly.

When we got married it was because my husband fulfilled me in ways that I'd never dreamt were possible. He was affirming, encouraging, supportive, loving, thoughtful, and lavished a great amount of attention on me. Because I had never experienced any of these things in all of my life, I ate it up! My husband became a god to me – perfect in all his ways. I think I can safely say that he held the same high opinion of me.

Then came the day when a "flaw" became evident. "No problem," I thought, and applied a little mental plaster over the blemish. "There! Good as new!" My perfect little god fell over once or twice. I mentally propped him back up, applied a little more plaster, and thought we were good to go. Where I found parts that I thought didn't belong in a god, I hacked and cut, trying to make him fit my image of what my god should look like.

This worked for a while; but then he got tired of being pushed around, fixed up, and cut on. Because he had been doing the same "remodeling" on me, rebellion began to set in as we fought to regain our original selves. We got tired of trying to fit into someone else's mold of what we should be like. We began clawing away the plaster to reveal the other's flaws and it got really ugly.

What on earth had gone wrong? Where had my god gone? How could I get him back? I knew that I needed him. How was I to fix this mess?

Isaiah 42:8 says, "I am the Lord, that is My name; and My glory I will not give to another, nor My praise to carved images." Could this be a hint as to what happened?

Is it possible that I had tried to substitute a man for God, and He was having none of it? Was it He who had turned our hearts from one another until we could learn Who was actually God…and who was not?

It has only been since I have been following the One True God, and allowing my husband to be human that I have seen things beginning to mend. As my relationship with God improves, and I look to Him to fulfill the deepest needs of my heart, He begins to turn our hearts back toward one another. The minute God sees me substituting my husband for Him, though, He allows my attempts to fail so I can remember that He will not share His glory with another, nor have His praise given to carved images.

That is what I had tried to do – to carve him into the image of what I wanted my god to look like.

First I tried with explanations of what I needed and why. When that didn't work, I tried manipulation and flattery to get what I wanted.

(An excellent definition of flattery: Insincerity with an agenda.)

Finally, I resorted to cutting remarks. Why I thought gashes and gaping wounds would make the other person look more god-like, I'll never know!

Have you experienced this in your marriage as well? Is it possible you're trying to get from your spouse that which only God can give? If you don't have a close relationship with the Lord, the answer is most likely, "yes."

Join me as I work daily to remember Who belongs on the throne of my life – and who belongs beside me…and to not confuse the two! As we do, the Lord will turn our hearts toward one another once again. Count on it.

LESSONS FROM LEAH

HER FATHER GAVE HER a name that meant, "weary." At least that wasn't as bad as her sister's name – "Ewe." Oh, yeah! Dad was on a roll!

Her wedding day came and the marriage was consummated. Imagine what happened when morning came. Do you suppose her husband reached over to snuggle with her, opened his eyes, then exclaimed, "*You*? What are *you* doing here? Where's your sister?" Did Jacob hear Leah's sobs as he stormed off in search of Laban?

However, it was too late. They were married...stuck. To make matters worse, Jacob returned later that day to announce that in a week he would be marrying her sister, Rachel. Pain must have shot through her already wounded soul. No one else had wanted her – and now Jacob didn't either.

Why hadn't she spoken up the night before? Was she desperate? Was she possibly jealous of Rachel? Had she hoped Jacob would see God's hand in this and realize the mistake he'd nearly made, and settle down to a contented life with Leah?

The Scriptures are silent on this, so all we can do is speculate. One thing was certain – the man who was to be her all-in-all didn't *want* her at all. I could weep for her pain and humiliation.

However, the *God Who Sees* saw her situation and had compassion on her. She bore a son to Jacob. The name she gave him speaks volumes. She called him Reuben, saying, "The Lord has surely looked upon my affliction. Now therefore my husband will love me."

Simeon came next, so named because "The Lord has heard that I am unloved." Her third son was named Levi. At his birth she said, "Now *this* time my husband will become attached to me, because I have borne him three sons."

Poor little Leah was looking for love and approval from a man who was either incapable, or unwilling, to give it.

As women, we expend huge amounts of energy trying to prove our worth to the world, our parents, spouse, families, or boss. We seem to work especially hard at getting approval and validation from those who cannot or will not tell us that we are OK. Every time we do something significant we run back to them asking, "how about now?" Unfortunately, like Jacob, they are so self-absorbed and insecure that they don't, or won't, notice. We go away to lick our wounds, determining to try harder next time.

What happened between the birth of Levi and Judah to shift Leah's focus? We don't know. Ah, but listen to her now. At the birth of her fourth son she said, "'now I will praise the Lord.' Therefore, she called his name Judah."

May we, like Leah, quit striving to gain the approval of other fallen humans and lift our eyes up to the One who made us and calls us by name. He is especially fond of you and sees you as holy, blameless, and above reproach! (Colossians 1:22)

Sowing and Reaping

AS NEWBORN BABES IN Christ, we crawl, then we toddle along, begin to walk...and finally learn to run. Paul tells us to run the race to win! There won't be a time in our lives for slowing down and kicking back spiritually – at least not until we leave this planet!

Psalm 1, however, warns us that if we slow to a walk we are in danger. The ungodly people around us like to talk. They like to share their opinions with us. They like to give their counsel. We hear them all around us. They're at the workstation next to ours, on our radios and TVs, at the store, and living next door.

They say things like, "Your children won't be happy unless you are happy. Do whatever it takes to be happy *for their sakes.*"

"Life is too short to be miserable. You only go around once, you know. You should get a divorce."

"Honey, you deserve to be treated better than that. He's a nice man. Go for it!"

"Live a little. Come party with us!" " Don't worry – be happy!"

"You deserve the best...just charge it. Deal with the bills later."

We need to run right on by these people.

If we don't, we'll soon find ourselves in their company..."standing in the way of sinners." Now this doesn't mean that they have to step over us. It means that we're on their road – on their turf. We look like them, we sound like them, and we act like them.

Before long, we will be sitting with them, laughing at those "silly Christians" who are running past us. We snigger at them and make fun of them for being "so heavenly minded that they're no earthly good." "If they'd just slow down for a bit they would see all the good times they're missing," we'd think to ourselves. We are sitting in the seat of the scornful.

We've gotten so used to the idea of grace that we don't get too disturbed if we commit a "little" sin here or there. After all, we've been forgiven. Now that we're on God's team, He will extend grace to us when we've had our fun and come back.

This is true. There isn't any sin we can commit that He can't forgive. But we're guilty of tucking 1 John 1:9 into our back pocket to apply when we need it, then doing whatever we want.

How I wish that this verse – the forgiveness of God – not only cleansed me from all unrighteousness, but wiped away *all* of the consequences as well. My worldly, religious friends left out a "little" piece of information when they assured me that God would wait patiently to forgive me, and welcome me back when I'd had enough.

It's another verse – Galatians 6:7 – that says, "Don't be deceived. God is not mocked. Whatever you sow you will also reap." This is *very* important for us to fully comprehend before we decide to "go walkabout" on God.

May I share *just one* "for instance" from my own life?

Most of you know that I've been divorced – not just once, but three times. I have children by all three of my ex-husbands. Do you understand that there is no way for God to undo what I have done without turning back the clock?

How would He reunite my family – realistically? Think about it.

Every husband had parents and siblings. They were (and still are) affected by the decisions that I made. Since we all got along during our marriage, our divorce hurt *them* as well. Try having family gatherings when your children have multiple sets of "grandparents." We usually end up celebrating holidays on a different day so that more of our children can join us.

Believe me, this is *not* about putting God in a box. There simply are too many people who were involved – whose lives would have to be drastically altered in order to undo the consequences of my actions.

Forgiven? Absolutely. Has God extended grace to me? There is no doubt in my mind that He has. Nevertheless, the consequences are something that I will have to live with for the rest of my life...and so will my children and grandchildren.

If you consider slowing down, consider this: before sowing "wild oats" it is wise to consider what sort of crop will be waiting for us at harvest time. "Tiny little" sins can end up really, really big. Behold the majestic oak and remember that it began as a *little* seed.

- 6 -

Lessons From Family

ARROWS AND QUIVERS

BEHOLD, CHILDREN ARE a heritage from the Lord, the fruit of the womb is a reward. Like arrows in the hand of a warrior, so are the children of one's youth. Happy is the man who has his quiver full of them. (Psalm 127:3-5a)

We moved to Orland, California in 1963 leaving behind everyone we knew. The only person we were related to here was my great-grandmother.

As a small child, I experienced the pain of leaving behind everyone I knew and loved. As an adult, I didn't want to go through abandonment again. I stayed near my parents.

However, when my own children married and had kids of their own, they *all* moved away! Pain shot through my heart as first one child, then another, then another, then *another*, left town, taking with them my beloved grandchildren.

Oh, the hours I spent crying out to the Lord about this loss! This went on for many months. I even used His Word to explain to Him what was wrong with this picture! My words seemed to fall on deaf ears.

One day, though, I began to consider arrows. What were they meant for? What purpose did they serve? Why would God liken them to children?

Picture a quiver in your mind. It's got seven arrows in it. It looks very nice like that, doesn't it? There's a lot of power in that person's armory. If I were a fighter, in search of a battle I'd look for someone with only one or two arrows, not a quiver full of them. Hmm.

As I continued to think about this word picture I began to see that an arrow might *look* nice all settled into its quiver, but it's not fulfilling what it was made to do. Arrows are designed to be fitted into a bow and sent out – away from its bowman. Some of them may be retrieved, but some never find their way back to the quiver.

Suddenly, I understood what was happening. My children, like arrows, had been sent forth into the world to make their mark. *This was the intent from the beginning!* I wasn't supposed to hang onto them indefinitely. Careful aim had been taken, and their flights had been true. They were now settled exactly where the Master Bowman had sent them. They had their own work to do in their predetermined destinations. My part of the process had ended. They no longer needed to be carried.

A sense of peace fell over me like nothing you could imagine. Things were going as they should. I hadn't been left behind because of some fault or other. This was exactly what they had been created to do, and they were doing it beautifully! God *is* still in charge – and knows what He's doing!

I watch for glimpses of them as they fly past now and again. I admire their flight – true and steady. Once in a while, one will land in our house for a brief visit, and then off they go again. Thanks for such precious gifts, Lord. They truly are my reward.

OBEDIENCE

"Tommy, stay out of the street!" his mother shouted. To her amazement, Tommy turned and applauded.

"Oh, that was great, Mom! You give excellent advice." Turning, he ran into the street, narrowly missed by the oncoming car.

"Tommy, take your clothes into your room and put them away," she told him as she headed back to the laundry room. Tommy obediently picked them up and put them away.

Later, she said, "Tommy. Stay out of the refrigerator. It's nearly mealtime and you won't be hungry when it's time to eat." Again, Tommy applauded.

"Wow! You think of everything. You really know a lot," he said as he popped another cookie into his mouth.

Now I ask you, what would *you* do with a child who behaved in such a way? We would be driven to distraction by one who picked and chose which orders he would obey. If he lived in my house, a trip to the woodshed would be in this young man's future!

As Christians, we have a heavenly Father who has given us His Word to follow and obey. Like Tommy, though, many of us pick and choose which commands we will follow and which ones we will ignore.

Why would we do such a thing? Could it be that we have not developed "an ear to hear?" We listen to sermons, but don't *hear* them. We walk away unchanged. We read the Word, but don't *hear* what God is telling us through it, and we get up from our devotions no different than when we opened the Bible.

Does this inability to hear God, which renders us ignorant of His commands, excuse us from obedience? The answer is "no." Just as ignorance of the law will not excuse us from being convicted of a crime, neither will ignorance *through inattention to God's Word* keep us from being disciplined. Ask the Israelites, who spent a great deal of time in the wilderness...eventually dying there!

Is it possible to read or listen without really hearing what's been said? The statement repeated seven times in Revelation says, "yes." The following verses all say the same thing: Rev. 2:7, 11, 17, 29; Rev. 3:6, 13, 22. It is this: "He who has an ear, let him hear what the Spirit says to the churches." If the command is *to hear* what has been said, then it would seem that it is entirely possible to *not hear* what is being said!

This would cause one to wonder if some of the trials we undergo are due to the fact that we have not developed a listening ear. Perhaps some of our struggles are a form of discipline that has been brought on by our picking and choosing which commands we will obey. David, in the Psalms, said, "to obey is better than sacrifice." We would do well to *hear* this, and take it to heart!

BLENDED FAMILIES

IN A BLENDED FAMILY, jealousy between the children is almost inevitable. Sooner or later, one child will state, "That's *my* dad. Don't you *ever* call him 'Dad'." The parents may not hear it, but it will be said.

In Ephesians 1:5 we read that "He (God) predestined us to adoption as sons through Jesus Christ to Himself, according to the kind intention (good pleasure) of His will."

We, as believers, are a blended family! We have the same, full benefits as if we were blood-related. Ephesians 1:11 states, "also we have obtained an inheritance, having been predestined according to His purpose who works all things after the counsel of His will."

I've met several elderly couples that chose to live together, rather than marry, in an effort to avoid the confusion of who inherits what when one of them dies. An inheritance is viewed as almost sacred.

Think about it. We are the adopted brothers and sisters of Jesus. Does He tell us, "That's *my* Dad, don't *ever* call Him 'Dad'"? No. In fact we read in Matthew 6:9, "Pray then in this way, '*Our Father...*'" In other words, "call Him 'Dad'. It's OK."

How does Jesus feel about sharing His inheritance – not with just one or two kids, but with billions? Ephesians 2:6-8 says, "who, although He existed in the form of God, did not regard equality with God a thing to be grasped, but emptied Himself, taking the form of a bond servant, and being made in the likeness of man. And being found in appearance as a man, He humbled Himself by becoming obedient to the point of death, even death on a cross."

John 14:2,3 says, "In My Father's house are many dwelling places...I go to prepare a place for you...that where I am, there you may be also."

Jesus is decorating your room!

He not only *knew* that He would share everything – even His own Father – but He did so willingly. He allowed Himself to be tortured and abused to the point where Mary, herself, could not recognize Him. He allowed Himself to become cursed (Galatians 3:13) by being crucified, and then to be separated from God.

As if sharing His Father and His inheritance were not enough, Jesus defends us. Romans 8:33,34 says, "who will bring a charge against God's elect? God is the One who justifies; who is the one who condemns? Christ Jesus is the one who died, yes, rather who was raised, who is at the right hand of God, who also intercedes for us." Hebrews 7:25 reads, "...since He (Christ) always lives to make intercession for them (those who are saved)." We have an Advocate (1John 2:1). We are free from condemnation (Romans 8:1,2) (See also Hebrews 9:24 and Romans 8:27)

We may be adopted into God's family, but we will *never* be greeted by arms opened wider, figuratively and literally, anywhere else!

Welcome to the most incredible family to which you will ever belong!

Happily Ever After

LIKE ME, DID YOU believe that when you were married you would live "happily ever after"? What a rude awakening I was in for!

It took many years for me to figure out that the primary purpose of marriage was to bring out the worst in me so I could surrender it to God, allowing Him to change me.

It took six kids for me to finally see that one of their functions was to model my own behavior for me to observe. They are such copycats!

How I wish someone had explained to me what God's purpose was for the institution of marriage. I'd like to think that I'd have cried, "Uncle" much sooner and a lot more often!

My husband served to bring out my self-centeredness, my controlling ways, and my desire to be the center of the universe. I wanted everything to revolve around me, and to be the queen of my domain.

My husband, however, had the same problems that I had. He was also self-centered, controlling, and wanted everything to revolve around him...to be the dictator who would be obeyed by all, without question.

Did the sparks fly? Oh, baby, I mean to tell you!

Of course, in the midst of our conflicts, there were my children showing me what I looked like. I couldn't understand why they didn't get along, why they were constantly cutting at one another, and so stinking selfish!

Every one of them was a "mini-Me" – and they were driving me crazy!

Little by little, I began to recognize bits of my own behavior in them. It was a real eye-opener.

Once I saw my behavior for what it was, I realized that I needed to have a heart-to-heart with my heavenly Father. I confessed my sins and submitted myself to the Holy Spirit for a major overhaul.

It's been several years since I first realized this and God has been faithfully working in me. He's not finished – not by a long shot! But He hasn't given up. Talk about patience!

Happily ever after? It's mine for the taking when I make the choice to *happily* give up what*ever* He is **after**!!

PERFECTIONISM

PERFECTIONISM DOES FUNNY things to people. What better child to exemplify this characteristic than one of my dear grandchildren?

For some reason, as an infant, he had a great need to do everything well. When learning to talk, he would practice in his crib – stopping the instant that he was aware of anyone within listening distance. When he was learning to walk and happened to fall, he would begin to examine the carpet carefully as if to make us believe that it had been done on purpose. His actions said, "I meant to get down here to see what this stuff is made of." It wasn't a fluke, a one-time thing! He did it consistently!

But the lesson here can be found in the adults around him. None of us thought less of him for his attempts. On the contrary! We expected him to stumble and fall, to use or say words incorrectly. We felt sorry for him because he was having such a hard time accepting that he was not perfect. We pitied him for the lack of grace he had toward himself.

Could it be that God feels the same way about us – His children – when we are silent toward Him for fear of misspeaking; or when we are standing still lest we risk walking and (oh, no!) fall? Does He pity me for my high expectations of myself – expectations that exceed even His?

I recall reassuring my grandson that it was OK to try and not succeed – that we already knew he wouldn't do everything perfectly...and loved him anyway. I'll bet if we were to get quiet with God, we would hear Him say something like this to us:

"My darling child, don't be so hard on yourself. You're not perfect and I know it. I never expected you to be. Don't you remember? I *made* you. I know what you're made of. My joy is in the effort, in your attempts to trust Me. I take pleasure when you try to be more like Me – just as you take pleasure in a little child's imitation of you when he's trying to learn to walk. I am pleased that you took the risk."

Don't fear failure. Fear the paralysis that sets in when you don't move, lest you fail. It's OK. Lighten up. Practice makes perfect as they say, but practice means risk. No matter how your attempts turn out, this will not affect My love for you."

I'm beginning to realize that we take ourselves far too seriously!

It is time to take off our fear of failure. It's time to quit worrying that we might be perfect in our attempts to serve God and serve others. We will never accomplish anything if we wait until we can execute things flawlessly.

May this be the year that we risk falling. Let's learn to laugh at ourselves when we tumble; and practice living fearlessly, daring to try. You'll feel more alive than you have in a long time!

When I am old and gray, I don't want to be sitting in my rocking chair with stories for my grandchildren of all the things I *could* have done. I want them to know that I *lived!*

- 7 -

Lessons In Identity

MY NAME IS TAMI

AN INTERESTING CHAIN OF events took place a few months after my mom's passing that would change my life forever.

The various tapes & CDs that I requested from Firefighters For Christ arrived that afternoon.

All of our sons were gone for the night.

While my husband was busy playing a game on the computer I looked through my new "talkie tapes" from FFC and selected a message by Frank Peretti. He is always good for a laugh and I wanted something light-hearted and unrelated to suffering. *What I Learned Since I Knew it All* sounded fun, so I put it in my player and began to listen to his message.

Mid-way through Frank's message, my husband decided to check e-mail. He told me that there were some messages there that I needed to read.

I figured that someone had responded to the message I posted to our home school e-loop earlier that day.

Lessons In identity

I was totally unprepared for what had come in. There were two e-mails from my youngest daughter, who had unexpectedly left town the week before my mother passed away. She left on a bus in the middle of the night, and I had no idea where she might have gone. At last, here was some correspondence from her. It was a relief to know she was still alive. With tears coursing down my cheeks, I replied.

I came back to finish listening to "Mr. Lighthearted"...only to have him take a turn to the serious side. He was speaking of Jacob, the supplanter, from Genesis 32:23. ("What is your name?" "Esau." "What is your name?" "First Born."). Jacob got into a wrestling match with the preincarnate Lord who touched his hip (so he couldn't run from God anymore), then asked him, "What is your name?" Finally giving up on claiming to be something he was not, he answered, "Just Jacob." That day, Jesus gave him a new name and a new destiny (Israel).

The story really hit home. My name is not "Home School Mom of the Year," "Spiritual Guru," "Super Wife" or any of the other identities I've taken on.

My name is Tami. Just...Tami. I sensed the Lord say, "Ah, good. Now I have something to work with!"

With that admission, I felt the weight of all the facades fall away. No longer did I need to try to pretend to be something I knew I wasn't. Maybe a few people were fooled by my attempts to imitate others, but the Lord wasn't. Not only that, but He wasn't pleased with my acts, either. He had created me to be me...exactly me...and no one else.

It is really hard to be the person God has created me to be when I work so hard at being someone else. A question I was asked once had a good point. It was this: "If I'm busy being someone else, then who is going to be me?" God wanted one of me in the world...not my best imitation of someone else!

What about you? Are you living life as the "real" you? Or are you giving your best imitation of someone else? God wanted *you* or He would not have made you. He is the one we must ultimately please. We *think* we have to please people, but we really don't!

God is glorified in a woman fully alive.

May our identity be found in You and You alone.

WHO AM I AGAIN?

ONE OF THE PHASES that I went through after the loss of my mother was that of trying to complete what I perceived to be her unfinished work. There were numerous half-finished projects – quilts, clothes, etc. and all of her fabric. I set out to take over where she left off, finishing her projects and making clothes for the grandkids.

When I realized that they weren't really "into" homemade, I turned my attention to making clothes for children in Nicaragua. I actually made many outfits, plus several dresses and tops for our missionary there.

When I finally stopped for a breath, I sensed God asking me what I was doing. I proudly told Him that I was finishing Mom's work. "She had unfinished work?" I sensed the question as if spoken aloud. "But, her work was done. I would not have brought her home, had her work on earth been incomplete."

Suddenly I realized that God had allowed me to see Mom finish her last "stitches" in the hospital. In her sleep, she had pulled up her sheet. With an imaginary needle and thread she "sewed" for quite a while. It was as if she were really sewing – right down to the little tug to pull the thread tight! At last, she tied a knot, cut the thread, put the needle into the pincushion, and smoothed the last thing she would ever "sew" here on earth. Although it had all been imaginary, it was meant as a gift from the Lord for my eyes only. Her work was finished.

As He reminded me of this scene, He let me know that sewing was her calling – not mine. What a relief this was – I *hate* to sew!

It is my responsibility to identify *my* calling and to pursue it. This has freed me from trying to fill positions left by people who either move away or pass on.

Who will fulfill God's call for *my* life if I am busy trying to be someone else? Every time I've caught myself trying to fill someone else's shoes, I suddenly realize that they pinch my feet! They are the wrong size because they weren't made for me. What a relief it is to take them off and put on my own! I've rarely enjoyed trying to fill someone else's call. It is hard work, unsatisfying, and joyless.

How gracious God is. He didn't slam-dunk me as I learned to find my way in a world that had drastically changed from what I'd previously known.

God is glorified in a woman fully alive.

Help me to be the woman You created me to be.

I AM NOT GOD

How one could be a music teacher and a psychiatrist at the same time is beyond me. As an eighteen-year-old, however, these were my career choices. Looking back, I'm not sure how that would have worked, but to my young mind, it was a great plan.

Being a mess internally, I had read numerous psychology books. I read secular works as well as Christian books on the topic. After a few years, I "knew" what was wrong with me and believed that I had a handle on it. Now I was ready to begin working on others.

It is a sad thing to tear into someone else's brokenness without the ability to bring healing to it. Unfortunately, this is what I did.

Time and again, I would "analyze" my subject, probing into their pain as I looked for the why of their problems. When nothing seemed to work, I left them a bloody mess and moved on to my next victim.

As time went on, I realized that I didn't have answers – for them or for me.

When I finally gave up my self-appointed call of healer, the Lord stepped in and began doing a work in me that continues to this day.

As Jehovah Rapha, the God Who Heals, I now know what true inner healing is. Unlike me, He doesn't dig into our pain for the sport of it, or because of a career choice. He comes with healing in His wings (Malachi 4:2). His is a healing that lasts!

In Luke 4: 18-19, Jesus says, "The Spirit of the Lord is upon Me, because He has anointed Me to preach the gospel to the poor; He has sent Me to heal the brokenhearted, to proclaim liberty to the captives and recovery of sight to the blind, to set at liberty those who are oppressed; to proclaim the acceptable year of the Lord." This is excellent news for us!

Are you spiritually destitute? Jesus wants you to know that you don't have to be. He came to offer you a rich spiritual life.

Are you brokenhearted? His desire is to mend it and make you whole.

Are you in bondage to anything: fear, habits, depression, and pride...anything at all? He offers liberty to you.

Are you spiritually blind? Have you lost your way? He is here to restore your sight.

What about oppression? What holds you back, keeping you from fulfilling the calling and using the gifts He has given? He offers freedom from all of that!

I pray that this will be the acceptable year of the Lord for you. (Another translation reads, "The year the Lord acts on your behalf.")

He has so much to offer you. Yes, He came to give you eternal life, but He also came to give you life to the full!

Lord, I am so thankful You have taught me that I do not have the ability to heal others, or to fix their problems. I'm sorry for presuming to be god to them. May I faithfully, henceforth, bring them to the One with "healing in His wings."

I am NOT a Rock

YOU CANNOT MOVE 15+ times in one decade and be unaffected by the frequent leaving behind of family and friends. Well—at least I couldn't.

Because of the death of my youngest brother and the belief that things were going to be better somewhere else, we never stayed in one place for very long. Just about the time I made new friends it was time to move again.

The first two months of fifth grade were spent in an elementary school in Martinez, California. We'd already been told that we were soon to move to Lafayette. Utterly heartbroken (I *loved* my school), I was "all ears" when my teacher introduced the song, *I Am a Rock,* by Simon & Garfunkel. The minute I heard that song I claimed it as the theme song for my life.

Maybe you remember the lyrics. It was full of self-protective statements, things like: build walls and a fortress so no one can get in; or, I don't need friends—they cause pain. Or these: I have books to protect me; or, shielded in my armor I'm untouchable and touch no one else. A rock feels no pain, and an island never cries.

Considering the number of people to whom I'd had to say, "good-bye," this song seemed full of sage advice to my little 10-year-old mind. Over the next 35 years, I comforted myself with its words again and again—crying less and less as my heart grew harder.

Meanwhile, I wondered why I always seemed to be on the outside looking in when it came to the women I knew. It seemed like I was the only one without friends. I just figured there was something desperately wrong with me. That must be why no one wanted me for a friend.

Praise the Lord! That ended a couple of years ago and I have many friends today.

Just last week, though, this song was brought to my attention and I realized that I'd made some 13 "agreements" in my pain and ignorance. Unwittingly, I'd set myself up to be a loner. While I felt rejected by everyone, the truth was that I had shut myself off. My walls—meant to protect me—had become my prison!

How thankful I am for Luke 4:18, 19 where Jesus stated that part of His mission was to set captives free!

As soon as I realized my grave error, I renounced every agreement I'd made through the song. What a relief to 'bust out' of captivity!

However, I'm wondering...am I alone in this? Or has someone else made this same mistake? Have you chosen a song, a poem, or a movie to define your life? Does it *really* reflect the life you want to live? If not, ask the Lord to replace it with His plan for you. After all, Galatians 5:1 says that it is for freedom that we have been made free! Let's live like it!!

"I have felt for the first time I can be myself– no more faces to hide behind; just a smile and a dream that's mine even if I am the only one who wants to fly."

(From *I'm Gonna Fly* by Amy Grant)

This is my new theme song. Much better, wouldn't you agree? Maybe you'd like to join me. I can tell you that being a rock stinks!

FROM ONE PHARISEE TO ANOTHER

IT'S SO RIDICULOUS that it's almost laughable. I look back on "those wretched religious folks." Well, not the folks, but what they taught and believed to be true. I sit on my self-righteous high horse and judge, judge, judge...especially now that I've reached a "higher level" of spiritual knowledge, and they're still stuck in the old stuff.

They had rules...lots of rules. "Do this. Don't do that." Christianity was like a straight jacket during those years. Those folks didn't have a very good understanding of grace. It was all about works.

I can get pretty arrogant with this, condemning them for not seeing it my way - in my *new* enlightenment! The next thing I know, I have the Sword out and begin hacking at them and trying to cut them down - if not out loud, then in my head.

(Of course when I do this I get hit in the head by the fruit they've produced. It falls all around me, evidence that they're not as dead as I thought them to be.)

Nevertheless, Jesus spoke on their behalf from the cross. He said, "Father, forgive them for they know not what they do."

What's this? His gaze is shifting. He's looking straight at me! He repeats His words so that there's no mistaking who He means.

"Yes, Lord. Here I am judging again, looking down on them for their ignorance. Yes, I know they're not the enemy. Then why am I using Your Sword on them? Well, uh... Yes, I see the fruit; but Lord, it's not peaches. If it's not peaches then it doesn't count! It does? Oh, ah... Yes, Sir. I'll put it away now and try to remember who my enemy really is!"

And dear old "Hairy" comes to mind once again, my dear friend in the front yard. It took me 10 years to get him to look that pathetic.

Imagine what people around me would be like if the Lord let me have my way with them! I can tell you from first-hand experience that an old oak, if limbed, will die. They're not meant to be pruned back that hard. The intense sunlight on their bared trunks is too much and they don't recover.

(This would explain the waist-high, dead trunk in my parent's front yard. It was cut back at my recommendation.)

Now that I think about it, I've learned a lot about God from landscaping! ... Mostly what NOT to do!

Lord, help me keep my eyes on You – and let You worry about everyone else!

In Jesus' Name,

Amen

- 8 -

Lessons From Deep In My Heart

SELF-RELIANCE

IN MY FAMILY OF origin, being a strong and self-reliant woman was a virtue to be praised; to need no one was a worthy goal. "I can take care of myself" was our motto.

This is all fine, well, and good except for one "minor" detail – God.

Jesus says, "Apart from me you can do nothing." Life experiences have shown me that I can do quite a lot.

God says, "I will supply all your needs." I'd reply, "Don't bother, I'll do it myself, thank You very much."

The Bible says, "Believe in the Lord Jesus Christ, and you shall be saved." My response was, "Are you kidding? I've put in 10 years teaching Sunday school, given my last dollar to the poor, and attended church regularly. I've earned myself a nice little condo by a lake in heaven. I'm working on a project right now that ought to allow me to upgrade to a small house with a couple of acres."

By the world's standards, self-reliance is a very positive character trait. By God's standards, it's a character flaw. That's right – a flaw.

Let's revisit the clay example used time and again in the Bible, but take a little different slant on it.

The more pliable the clay, the easier it is to shape. When it begins to harden, moisture is required to soften it up again. If the medium is clay, the moisture used is water. If the medium is a human heart, the moisture required is tears. The harder the medium, the more moisture is required. If it's too hard, it must be pulverized to make it useable again.

It has taken many years to realize that being self-reliant is not in my best interest. It leaves no room for dependence upon God. Because of my ignorance, He's had to allow me to be pulverized many times to bring me to the place where He could begin molding me into His image.

How I wish I had chosen little tears of thanksgiving for His strength. These would have kept me malleable. Instead, I chose buckets of tears, cried in grief, to bring me to the place where I would admit I couldn't stand on my own. It is much easier to rely on God for everything I need.

ATTITUDE IS EVERYTHING

IT WAS A COLD 41°F, and my sons and I were broken down in the midst of the strawberry fields outside Doris, California. To make matters worse, we were not dressed for the cold. When we'd left Redding that morning, it was 80°F. My initial reaction was not pretty. I did the usual stuff most folks do when cars break down, I'm sorry to say.

We assessed the situation and tried to figure out the most likely place to find a phone. (I still haven't joined the cell phone generation!) We decided to head for the Forest Service building a couple of miles down the road. As we walked, I got the boys to join me in some praise songs. We made an adventure of it.

We'd only gotten a few hundred yards down the road when a woman stopped to ask if we needed to use her cell phone. To my dismay, all I got was my husband's message box. I explained where we were as best I could, and then planned to walk back to the car. This sweet lady, though, had a better idea. Why didn't we come home with her and try calling again?

It was a very pleasant afternoon. We were fed and cared for. They were a great Christian family. She didn't normally stop for people alongside the road, but had sensed the Lord telling her to do so that day.

After we had been there a few hours, I was suddenly amazed at how my choice earlier had affected this day. Had I remained in my foul mood, she would never have considered taking us home. We would have had to wait in the car for the five hours it took for Wendel to come get us...in the freezing cold. Instead, I was enjoying a wonderful time of fellowship with a sister in the Lord in a warm house with a full stomach.

Either way – bad attitude or good attitude – my car was still sitting alongside the road, broken down. I learned a valuable lesson that day, one I try to use often. I don't always succeed, but I am getting better.

This choice of attitudes works in all sorts of situations: relationship conflicts, crises, and financial situations – you name it.

Once we realize that God is in control – all the time – and believe it, resting in Him and waiting expectantly to see how He is going to work in it becomes easier. However, if we never risk trusting Him we can live an entire lifetime without knowing this truth experientially. How sad!

The first few times it's really scary, but after a while it comes almost naturally. (Except for the really "BIG" things...I still have to work hard to rest when it comes to those!!!). In Romans 12:2 the command is for us to be transformed by the renewing of our minds. This means to think less like a human and more like a loved child of God. It means leaving behind the world's way of handling things, setting aside manipulation, and putting our hands down as we wait upon the Lord. We surrender ourselves to the Lord and ask Him to show us what He desires to change in us through the trial. He *does* desire to change something or He would not have permitted the test in the first place.

"This all sounds good, but how can we do this," you ask? By putting Philippians 4: 8,9 to work. Find something around you that is good, just, pure, lovely, or praiseworthy and shift your thoughts to that. Some days, for me, the only thing I can think of at the moment is that the sun faithfully rose, or that I have a roof over my head and plenty to eat.

There's always *something* to be thankful for if we will look for it, so thank God for it and do it out loud!! Then find something else, and then something else. In no time at all, you'll be in a much better mood – and a better frame of mind to handle whatever is going on.

Stuff happens around us – people act badly, things go wrong, and troubles are inevitable. The truth is that they happen *around* us, and not *in* us. Others may be able to affect our environment, but they can never affect our hearts and minds *unless we allow them to.* That's right! We have to give them permission to "make us feel" however it is we are feeling. Why do I want to give someone else that power over me? No thanks.

Once we begin to choose what kind of attitude we will have, we won't want to live like a victim – subject to our circumstances and people – anymore. This is truth that sets us more free than we ever thought possible!

Dan Crawford said it well: "Jesus said, 'Let's go to the other side of the lake;' not, 'Let's go to the middle of the lake and drown!' With Jesus in our boat we can smile at the storm." What a great reminder for all of us.

The next time you're facing something unpleasant, *choose* a good attitude. You'll be glad you did!

THE CRITICAL JUDGE

LAST JULY I WAS sitting on the beach picking up shells and minding my own business. At least I thought I was. Then the Holy Spirit brought to mind the topics of my thoughts over the last half hour! I began to see that I'd spent a fair amount of time thinking about different people – either criticizing or judging them.

For the first time in my life I realized how mentally exhausting that was!

To my embarrassment, I had been using myself as the standard by which I was making my calls. Those I deemed "worse" than myself I judged for their lack of maturity – spiritual or otherwise. Those I deemed "better" than myself I picked apart until I found something I could criticize – you know, cut them down to my size. Dare I admit...sometimes this was aimed toward God?

Since then I have been paying attention to this tendency of mine and I find that it isn't limited to family, friends, and fellow believers. Rather, I have set myself up as judge over the world! I judge the person who cut me off as "stupid"; the one who pushed me out of the way at the store as "rude and selfish", etc.

Phil. 4:6,7 says, "in everything by prayer and supplication with thanksgiving let your requests be made known to God; and the peace of God, which passes understanding, shall keep your hearts and minds in Christ Jesus." That is what I had been missing – opportunities to lift others up in prayer, thanking God for them. Most importantly, I had missed out on peace!

The older I get the more I value peace – peace of mind and inner tranquility. Up to now, I always believed that my lack of peace was everyone else's fault! *They* were robbing me of my peace. Now I understand that I do it to myself by my judgmental and critical spirit.

Having become aware of this I have asked the Lord to "tap me on the shoulder" every time I let my mind drift into a critical or judgmental mode.

As I'm bringing more of my thoughts into captivity to the obedience of Christ, I find that I am less tired mentally and more peaceful – no matter what is going on around me. I can be still and let God run the universe. When I obey the Word and focus on "whatever things are good, right, just, lovely, praiseworthy, etc." (Philippians 4:8) I find loving others is so much easier.

Ephesians 4:29 says to "let no unwholesome thing proceed out of your mouth, but only such a word as is good for edification according to the need of the moment, that it may give grace to those who hear." This has become much easier…and it should, for Matthew 12:34 says, "out of the abundance of the heart the mouth speaks." When I'm not dwelling on what is wrong with everyone around me, I don't have negative things to say. My thoughts feed my words…as well as my actions.

My goal is to turn my "observations" of others into prayer and thanksgiving so that I may relax into the peace of God, which passes all understanding.

Papa, thank You for pointing this out to me. Help me to guard my heart and mind against anything that would keep me from loving others with Your love.

In Jesus' Name, Amen.

SELF-EXALTATION

DID YOU KNOW THAT the "kissing cousin" of criticism and judgment is self-exaltation? As I've pondered this, I realized that it's a sneaky sin. It's easy to do, and is so much a part of my life that I was shocked when I realized how often I was guilty of it.

It happens every time I tell "my side" of the story. I'm good with words...aren't we all when we're explaining how good we are – and how bad they are? However, even as I am recounting the events there's a little voice inside of me saying, "Whoa! You stretched *that* one a lot, didn't you?" or "Yeah, that's what *they* did/said, all right...right after *you* said/did...."

You know, if you're quick enough you can squelch that voice before the sentence is completed. Then your conscience doesn't bug you too much!

There is a little verse tucked away in Ezekiel 16:8 that convicts me whenever I "confess" someone else's sin *for* them. It reads, "I saw that you were at the time for love, so I covered your nakedness with my skirt." You see, whenever I am exposing someone else's faults I am not being loving to them. I am never less like Christ, who deals with me privately, than when I am revealing someone else's sin.

The Bible says that if we exalt ourselves we *will* be humbled, but if we humble ourselves He will exalt us in due time. This is so important that it's found in 1 Peter 5:6 and James 4:10.

I can talk a good talk and present the "facts" in such a way that I appear to be blameless. You too, hmmm? I believe Hitler was the one who said, "If you tell a lie long enough and loud enough, people will come to believe it as truth." When I tell my story repeatedly, in my mind it becomes the truth. However, there is a day of reckoning coming.

Luke 14 is an exhortation to "not think more highly of ourselves than we ought" (Romans 12:3), but to humbly seek a lower place at the table. If I believe my own press about conflicts, I will proudly take a seat near the head of the table. Imagine how humiliating it would be to have the Lord ask me to move, then replace me with the very ones I had been in conflict with during my life. After all, He knows the truth in *every* situation – no matter how well and convincingly I present my "facts"! I'm pretty sure that "Humble Pie" is served to those seated at the other end!

Father, lead me into *all* truth – especially about myself. Please show me when I am exalting myself.

In Jesus' name, Amen.

- 9 -

Lessons To Remember

IN LIFE'S TUMBLER

ROCK POLISHING IS A lengthy process. It requires only a few things: a tumbler, four types of abrasives, water, and stones. Some of the steps are repeated until finally the inner beauty of the stone shines through.

We recently went to Stone Lagoon on the Pacific Coast by Orick, California to look for agates. As we were standing on the beach of seemingly-gray stones, a wave broke upon the shore and soaked them. Suddenly they glimmered like jewels. It was beautiful to behold.

As I stood there, I realized that life is like a rock tumbler. We're rough and dull, pitted and unshapely. Suddenly, we are tossed into the tumbler with others who are just like us, along with an abrasive (also known as a trial). The machine is turned on and round and round we go, being ground by the grit and by one another!

When He judges the process to have been at work long enough, the Master Tumbler stops the spinning, opens the container, and dumps out the contents. One by one, He inspects each stone to see if it's been sufficiently smoothed or needs more work. If it needs more time being worked with the coarsest abrasive, more stones are added. The tumbler is reloaded and the tumbling process begins again.

If it's been adequately smoothed, the stone goes into a pile with others like it. A different abrasive is added and the next phase of tumbling begins. Think of this as a different sort of trial.

Back and forth the stones are piled, smoothed, and inspected until – at last – they are ready for the polish. I like to think of polishing as being done with a liquid and a soft cloth. This would turn stones into dust magnets, though! Oh no, it takes another very fine abrasive to give rocks that beautiful shine.

As I looked at the stones around my feet I realized that this is life. It's all about being rubbed, tossed around, ground on, and sanded. With time and tumbling, we are worn smooth. With each step, we become more like the Lord until we develop the shine of His glory, and become His beautiful gems.

The tumbler can mean different things to different people – or in different stages of their lives. The tumbler can be life in general, a work situation, a marriage, health, or even our church fellowship! The rocks in the container represent other people who are in the situation with us; they can also represent several problems hitting us all at once. The water is the hand of God positioning us to get the most benefit from the process.

There have been many times when I've wanted to shout, "Stop the world, and let me off!" It turns out that I just wanted Him to stop the tumbler and *let me out*; but a glance back at what I was like then, and who I am slowly becoming, makes me thankful for the process. I can see results!

So, when someone seems to be rubbing you the wrong way, praise the Lord because that's what he or she is supposed to do. Proverbs 27:17 reads: "As iron sharpens iron, so a man sharpens the countenance of his friend." Not a very happy thought, but necessary nonetheless!

But we have this treasure in earthen vessels, that the excellence of the power may be of God and not of us. We are hard-pressed on every side, yet not crushed; we are perplexed, but not in despair; persecuted, but not forsaken; struck down, but not destroyed.

1 Corinthians 4:7 – 9

GIVE AND GET

LUKE 6:38 SAYS, "Give, and it shall be given unto you; good measure, pressed down, shaken together, and running over will be put into your bosom, for with the same measure that you use, it will be measured back to you."

We read this and say to ourselves, "Ooh! I'm going to give money to the poor, food to the S.O.U.P. ministry, and clothing to the park ministry. Cool! Watch how God gives back to me!"

There's truth in this. God does not necessarily repay us in goods, but we find the attitudes of our heart being returned to us in many ways through the kind acts of others.

However, why don't we read the verse right before it? This one says, "Judge not, and you shall not be judged. Condemn not, and you will be forgiven." The very next verse is the one that says, "Give..." That puts a different slant on the verse.

Giving good things to others is easy, and it's fun. It's the most satisfying thing that I've ever done. I always come away feeling happier and more joyful.

Isn't it true, though, that judging and condemning others also comes easily? It provides its own sense of satisfaction and self-righteousness. I've left some "bashfests" feeling downright good about myself. When we've finished ripping someone to shreds verbally (who's never there to defend themselves... *why is that?*), it's easy to feel superior and holier-than-thou!

Why is it that we don't apply our "give, and it shall be given to you" verse here? Due to the close proximity of the verse on judging and condemning to this one – and the fact that it appears between the section on loving our enemies and the parable of the splinter and the log – it *has* to apply to these things as well.

Remember back in the late '80s and '90s when the whole "dependent/co-dependent" movement became popular...when it was fashionable to dissect our parents' treatment of us? Oh, yeah, baby! Let me tell you, I had a field day.

It wasn't until years later that I discovered the principles of "give and it shall be given" and "whatever you sow, that will you also reap." As I ignorantly modeled how to dishonor parents, there were 7 little pairs of eyes watching my every move. Yes, 14 little ears taking in my every word.

Another thing I learned is that the passing on of sin to the third and fourth generation is not a curse of *God*, but rather is the reality that children live what they learn. Most children grow up to repeat what they've seen their parents do, and also what has been done to them. God had nothing to do with that – except to warn us about what would happen.

My children have shown me the truth of this. I passed a lot of judgments on my folks, and condemned them many times. Why was I so surprised when my dear children didn't honor me any more than I had my own parents?

At first, I didn't understand what was going on. I'd given immense love to them, provided for them materially, encouraged, and supported them. When some of them turned on me, I was devastated. How could they do such a thing after everything I had done for them?

The not-so-nice part I'd rather leave out is that a few years prior, they had witnessed me dishonoring their fathers, as well as my own mom and dad. They were living what they had learned...and I was on the receiving end of the deal.

In Amos, the Lord promises to give back the years that the locusts have eaten, and I am so thankful that this is finally coming to pass for me. One by one, my relationships with my adult children are being restored. It's touch-and-go right now – but that's mostly because I'm guarding my heart. As I have been taking risks and letting them back in we are repairing the breaches and God is blessing us.

Therefore, we need to be very careful what we're dishing out – we will get it back by the truckload!

GRACE – THE GIFT THAT KEEPS ON GIVING

"GRACE TO YOU AND peace from God our Father and the Lord Jesus Christ." Paul used this as a standard salutation in all his letters.

This is something that I've always taken to mean that by finding grace through Christ's sacrifice, we have peace with God, but today I saw this in a new light.

It began with a car that had been parked by an "idiot" at the store. As I pulled in, I wondered what kind of Bozo would park like that! When I got back to my car it was still there, parked "all wrong" for *the entire* world to see. To my shame, I toyed with the idea of waiting for the driver to come out so I could see what kind of moron would do this! Suddenly I realized that it was such a silly thing to get worked up over, and let it go.

That's when I saw it! The instant I extended grace and gave the driver permission to do something (gasp!) wrong, I experienced peace.

When I think of the countless days I've spent replaying the jerks who have cut me off, cut in front of me, or otherwise infringed on what was "rightfully" mine, I feel so foolish.

Am I alone in my self-centeredness? I don't think so – and I can prove it with magazines.

When I was a kid "Time" and "Life" were the top magazines. By the time I was in my 20's, the rage was "People" and "Us." One of today's top sellers is named – you guessed it – "Self!"

The problem with this is that the more self-centered we become, the less willing we are to extend grace to others. Consequently, the less grace-full we are toward others, the less peace we have.

Imagine how different we would be if instead of getting angry at the rude driver who cut us off we gave them the benefit of the doubt and prayed for them. They *could* be hurrying to the deathbed of a loved one. Maybe they cut in front of us at the store because they were anxious to get home and care for a sick spouse or child. Perhaps the Lord allowed their thoughtlessness (and He *did*, you know!) to bring that person to our attention so that we could pray for their salvation.

Oh, life is *so* not about us!!!

This year, in addition to material presents, we could give the gift of grace to all we meet. If we freely bestow on others the grace to be less than perfect – human, even…to be "*tenderhearted, forgiving one another even as God in Christ forgave us*" (Ephesians 4:32) not only will we enjoy greater peace, but in this "me" world we will be obviously different.

May we go gently through this holiday season and the upcoming New Year, leaving behind the fragrance of Christ to a lost and dying world.

May your light shine brightly as you dispense grace liberally; and may the peace of God be yours to enjoy in abundance through Christ our Lord. Amen.

THE JOY OF THE LORD

WITHOUT A DOUBT, I was in the midst of the hardest time of my life.

It began when my mother's angiogram revealed four blockages of her heart, requiring immediate surgery. The surgery went well, but a week later, she was back in the hospital with kidney stones that couldn't be removed because of the blood thinners she was taking.

Stressed family members handled this in different ways, either leaving or lashing out at others. Things didn't improve and my mom moved to heaven, leaving chaos in the wake of her absence.

During the six months surrounding her death, I sustained the loss of 13 relationships, many of them family members who didn't cope well with the situation. Among them were those who left town, those who chose me to be the recipient of their tongue-lashings, relationships that have, for the most part, remained in tatters. I also had two dear friends die during that time.

About four months into this nightmare, some well-meaning Christians asked me, "Tami, where is the joy of the Lord?"

"Happy?" I spat my words at them. "You want *happy?* I can't go there right now. I don't even remember what 'happy' looks like, but 'joy'...I've got joy. Joy is the *rock-solid* conviction that, even in the midst of all that is going on, God is *still* on His throne and He is *still* in control. It looks ugly, but God is doing His mighty work in all of this. *That* is my joy."

In that moment, I sensed a calm come over me like nothing I have ever experienced. Being put on the spot like that, I had finally defined joy in a way that made sense.

I could finally be free to mourn the losses, to grieve, to sit in Papa's lap and sob my heart out. I didn't have to put on my "happy face" and pretend to the world that I had been unmoved by what was taking place around me. I could be as real as the pain I felt. It was OK to feel it. In that response was truth that I could cling to, given to me by the Holy Spirit who was there to comfort me.

Something inside me shifted that day; an amazing change took place.

Things continued to be a painful mess for a couple of years afterward, but I was able to walk through the difficulties with a sense of peace and calm. This truth spoken *to* me, as it was spoken *through* me, became the source of my strength. Time and again, I would remind myself that God was still in control – even in the midst of the greatest storm of my life.

He held me secure like an anchor.

Through the joy of the Lord, I was able to reach out in love to those around me and minister to them. I was able to comfort others who were mourning.

Most importantly, I was able to keep "engaged" with God. The joy of the Lord gave me strength so that I didn't fall back on my old way of coping, which was to crawl into a bottle of alcohol and come out when things had improved. He was my Rock, my Shelter, my Strong Tower, and in Him I found rest.

What's your storm right now? Is it problems in your marriage? Is it wayward kids who are beyond your reach? Are your finances causing distress? Whatever you are facing,

God is still in control and He is working behind the scenes for your good. He *can* be trusted.

You wait, you watch, you'll see. The Lord's joy *is* your strength.

- 10 -

Lessons Of Beauty

LIFE AS A MUSICAL SCORE

MUSICIANS ARE OCCASIONALLY asked to play a piece of music "cold," that is, something they've never seen (or maybe even heard) before. A well-trained artist will take a few minutes to look over the score before beginning. Some of the things that will be noted are: speed, loudness, what key it's played in, tempo changes, sections that will be repeated, etc. Having prepared in this way, the musician has a much better chance of playing it well.

As Believers, our lives are like sight-reading. We've been given a life to live and we're to play it "cold." The tempo of our lives will change, sometimes going very quickly and at others trudging along at a snail's pace.

The volume of our lives will also change. Sometimes it's a shout for joy, the cry of pain, the thundering rage of trials, or the whisper of a prayer.

There will be key changes along the way. Sometimes we are in the major key of the mountaintop. At other times, it will change to the minor key as we go through the valley of the shadow of death.

Sometimes we feel like we are in a squirrel cage, as we seem to be repeating the same scenarios again and again. At other times, we will return to the beginning of relationships or situations and try to start over.

We have a "score" before us, a part in God's grand composition. Moreover, we have "recordings" of how others have played before us. If we read through and listen to it carefully we will be better prepared for the changes that will come our way – for there are two things that *never* change – God, and the fact that everything else changes!!!

We can "hear" the music before we are required to play it, as we "listen" to the masters go before us – David, Rebecca, Joshua, Job, and the rest.

We can follow along with Moses as he lives out the slow, quiet pace of his youth; we hear the increase in tempo and volume as he strikes down the Egyptian guard, the whisper of trying to cover what he has done. There's the long, slow section while he spends 40 years in Midian tending sheep. The pace increases, as does the volume, when he returns to Egypt to confront Pharaoh and demand the release of his people. The next section plays like craziness as plagues come and go and the people prepare for their departure. Hear the staccato of the people rushing away from Egypt, the frenzy of being cornered at the Red Sea. The music swells and is accented by the cymbal crash of the parting of the water.

On and on it goes – the "repeats" as they take another lap around Mt. Sinai (40 years-worth!), "take it from the top" sections as they repent and return to God, until, for Moses the piece comes to a close.

As we study Moses & the Israelites, we can "hear" how they played the score given to them and note things that we would do differently. We see the faithfulness of the Composer as He conducts the players through their part of His grand piece. We will be better equipped to play our part if we heed the instructions for each section, knowing that one great day we will at last come to the word we long for – Fine. The End.

Oh, that we will hear on that day, "Well done, good and faithful servant. Enter into the joy of the Lord!"

TRUE WORSHIP

I WAS IN LOVE and everyone could tell by the transformation that took place almost overnight! There was a new spring in my step, a glow on my face, and a carefree cheerfulness that hadn't been there before.

My daily chores took on new significance. They were no longer just a list of things that had to get done; now they were acts of service for the one I loved. I cooked the foods I knew he liked best, and dressed in a manner that would please him. I vacuumed, swept, dusted, and scrubbed with him in mind. When shopping I wanted him to see what a good steward I was with money.

Day and night, I thought about him. We talked frequently during the day and spent our evenings together. My schedule was effortlessly rearranged to allow for maximum time together. Hours apart seemed like an eternity!

In short, everything I did was for him and with him in mind. The term "good enough" disappeared from my vocabulary. You could say that everything about me was an act of worship for my beloved.

What a lot we could learn about worship from falling in love.

Let me quote William Barclay and maybe it will make more sense: "
'So,' Paul says, 'take your body; take all the tasks that you have to do every day; take the ordinary work of the shop, the office, the factory, the shipyard, the mine, (the home); and offer all that as an act of worship to God...'

"True worship is the offering to God of one's body and all that one does every day with it. Real worship is not the offering to God of liturgy, however noble, and a ritual, however magnificent. *Real worship is the offering of everyday life to Him.*"

You see, worship – true worship – is not *just* what we do on Sunday morning before the sermon. As Rory Noland puts it in *The Worshipping Artist*, "If worship is giving all of ourselves to God, then everything we do is potentially an act of worship. We are instructed to acknowledge the Lord in all we do (Proverbs 3:6). So how we live our lives is how we praise God." (p.27)

(As an aside: Perhaps this is why the Lord never puts anyone in our lives who can meet all our needs. If He did, we would have no need for a relationship with Him).

Imagine the impact we would have on the world around us if we were to fall madly and passionately in love with the Lord! Those who know us would be able to see the transformation. It might stir in them a longing for the same.

Such a relationship with Him takes time…remember how much time, and what kind of attention we lavished on courtship? He is worth it – oh, He's worth every ounce of effort we're willing to put forth!

My prayer is that we would fall so head-over-heels in love with our Lord that our lives would be transformed as we do everything with Him in mind. When we live every part of our lives out of a desire to please our Beloved we will be true worshippers.

LOST DREAMS

WHAT DID YOU DREAM of becoming when you were little? Are you living out that dream or did you give up and settle for something more "sensible?"

As a child, I loved music. I lived, slept, ate, and breathed music. It was my most intimate way of connecting to God.

I had an enemy who knew that.

Although an accomplished musician by the time I was 18, I sang for the last time when I was 19. Hurt followed hurt until I decided that it wasn't worth it. Besides, I was told to do something "useful" with my life. Music was seen as a selfish hobby by the adults around me, rather than viewed as my calling.

Bayles & Orland wrote a book entitled *Art and Fear*. In it they state, "in the end it all comes down to this: you have a choice...between giving your work your best shot and risking that it will not make you happy, or not giving it your best shot – and thereby *guaranteeing* that it will not make you happy." (p. 68)

Where were these guys when I was younger? Why couldn't someone have told me this a whole lot sooner?

Rory Noland's book, *Thriving as an Artist in the Church* was also insightful. In the section entitled, *You Need Your Art*, he states, "whether you realize it or not, you need your art. Your skill level is not important. For most of us engaging in our art is like therapy. When David wrote, 'My soul yearns, even faints, for the courts of the Lord; my heart and flesh cry out for the living God' (Psalm 84:2) he was using music to express the depths of his soul. As it was with

David, our art can be cathartic. It can help us sort out our deepest thoughts and feelings, and it is critical for our spiritual health and well-being. It can sustain us through struggles and hardship.

"If you've put your talent on hold for one reason or another, I invite you to take it up again, if for no other reason than that you need your art...

"...One night at the piano was all it took for this man to rediscover the joy and meaning that music could add to his life."

I can honestly say that I never felt more alive than when making music —either alone or with others. It's the best thing in the world! When I look back at all the years that I'd shelved my music, it is with a great deal of regret.

On the other hand, there's also a lot of anticipation, because one of heaven's great delights will be music – perfect, pure music!

Although the wasted years can't be undone, I *can* begin to fulfill the calling to which I have been called – to sing praises to the One who deserves all of my praise. I can sing when the mood strikes...wherever I may be; at the store, pumping gas, at home, anyplace. I can set aside all of my silly rules about it and just enjoy it for what it is...the joy of my heart spilling over my lips and onto those around me.

What about you? What is that thing that left you feeling fulfilled like nothing else? Do you still enjoy it? Or have you given it up for more "sensible" or "productive" activities? It came as a surprise to me to discover that we are called "human beings," not "human doings." Our primary function is to *be* in a relationship with God...in whatever form that may take, rather than to be *doing* "religion" for Him!

We need to be in communion with the Lord, doing that special thing He put inside us. It was a gift designed to enhance our time with Him. It may seem to be a waste of time, or silly, but if it draws us closer to our Creator then it's a good thing. Let's revive some dreams!

HOPE

To the cupboard I went in search of hope,
For that last little bit in the jar.
There it was in its own little niche
But I'd long ago emptied that jar.

"Where, oh where can I get some hope?"
(It can't be bought in a store)
"I needed so little," I frantically plead,
"Please tell me where I can get more."

"If you will just trust Me and rest in My care,"
I heard that small voice in my head,
"I'll lead you and guide you to where you must go.
On your plight some light I will shed."

"Then lead me," I cried, "and I'll surely go.
As you see my heart's full of despair.
My own strength and hope I've completely used up.
I've no choice but to trust that You care."

As we went on our way He gently explained,
"There is no hope to be found
In stores, or in cupboards, or within yourself.

This you know for you've looked all around.

"If you're to find hope I know just where to take you.
To others, who just like yourself,
When searching to find their last little drops
Found a mere empty jar on their shelf."

"If their jars are empty, then why do You lead me
To them?" I cried, "You said, 'trust!'"
"But their stores are no longer vacant," said He.
"To go to them is a must."

"For you see, when they found their jars to be void
Of hope…they found the key.
Another shared how her life had been brought
From the depths – to heights walked with Me."

"It's only through caring and sharing, you know,
That another's hopes will be raised.
Then when your hope-jar is filled to the brim
There's only Me to be praised."

And the things that thou hast heard of Me among many witnesses, the same commit thou to faithful (wo)men, who shall be able to teach others also. 2 Timothy 2:2

THE BELOVED PRINCESS

A NOBLE WOMAN IS one who is a child of the King – and knows it. She walks with her head up, for who would dare condemn the king's daughter She is secure in her Father's love and knows that she is loved because she "is," not because she "does."

She has dignity and is gracious, both in word and deed. She speaks to others in the same manner as her Father speaks to her – gently, lovingly, softly, and kindly. Her words build up, never condemn, and never judge, for she knows it is only the King's responsibility to judge – never her own.

Her dress is fitting for her position. It needn't be cheap or scanty in an effort to draw attention to herself.

This woman has "presence," and in a world where everyone hurries and scurries her quiet and gentle spirit draws people much like an oasis draws nomads. She is serene, and that is attractive to those who are constantly harried.

She spends much time in her Father's presence, so she learns wisdom at His knee. As she brings her problems and cares to Him, she learns how He thinks and how consistent He is. She then emulates Him. Her goal is to grow up to be "just like Daddy." She willingly gives up her wants in order to do that which she knows her Father would prefer.

Obedience is something she knows to be of utmost importance. Obeying Father keeps her from making painful mistakes. It also frees her from the guilt and consequences disobedience brings. For although her Father is loves her, He is also just. He has no favorites among His children;

therefore, misdeeds do not go undisciplined. Ah...but she also knows His forgiveness!

The princess would not consider gossip for one moment, lest it dishonor the King. Temper tantrums are out of the question, as are cursing and making light of her King or His position. Purity in all matters is an absolute must, for she is a child of the Almighty God, and she knows He is deeply grieved when her heart harbors sin.

To be a worthy daughter of such a King requires discipline. It is much easier to do what she wants, what her "flesh" demands. Yet, she knows that to give in is to separate herself from her Father. The peace and security of living as a princess, when weighed against the fear and pain of the life of a rebel, cannot compare.

The worth of the princess is "*Jesus*"...for that is how much the King paid as her ransom.

She is <u>truly</u> priceless.

About the Author

Tami describes herself as a "missionary cleverly disguised as a homemaker." She lives in Redding, CA, with her husband, Wendel. They have 7 children and 9 grandchildren.

"This book is a dream come true for me," she says. "I've waited all my life for permission to write it. I don't know whose approval I thought I needed to have, so I've decided to set aside the fear of being in trouble for doing this without 'their' OK. If 'they' come yell at me, at least I'll know who 'they' are! I can be so silly sometimes!"

A member of Valley Christian Fellowship's worship team (under the direction of Bill King), one of her greatest pleasures is worshipping our Lord in song. Another is in-depth Bible study. "God's Word has to be the most fascinating book of all time. Every detail has a purpose, and fits so perfectly with every other part of the book. It is intricately woven together like the finest tapestry, and is found woven into my own life. What an amazing God we serve!"

She can be contacted via e-mail at

batransformed1@yahoo.com.

Thank you for taking the time to read this book. I'd love to hear from you!

In His Majesty's service,

Tami

\o/

Praise Him!

Lessons by Heart

Lessons by Heart

Benson

Learned at the Feet of Jesus

by Tamara J. Benson

Like the pearls of a beautiful necklace, so are the days of our lives. Each one was carefully selected for our personal strands...

Imagine what a surprise the first pearl discovery must have been! It was most remarkable, to be sure; such a beautiful find in a most unlikely place. As they held it up to the light, no doubt they were awestruck at the hues of purple, gold, and blue that shimmered from its surface.

Isn't that what life is like? In the midst of some of the ugliest circumstances we discover little nuggets of beauty.

During our stay on earth we are given a series of object lessons. As they are strung together, they become our adornment – not unlike a strand of pearls.

When we hold them up to the Light, we find the fingerprints of Jesus – purple, and gold, and blue – all over them!

Come with me and examine a few of the pearls I have acquired from a half-century of living. My greatest joy has been discovering that God was present in the creation of each one. He has been carefully crafting a work of art.

It is His masterpiece. To God be the glory!!

$13.98
ISBN 978-0-578-02735-7

www.ingramcontent.com/pod-product-compliance
Lightning Source LLC
LaVergne TN
LVHW091306080426
835510LV00007B/386